Beyond the Flesh: The Ethics of Enhancement

joseph demegillo

Published by joseph demegillo, 2024.

While every precaution has been taken in the preparation of this book, the publisher assumes no responsibility for errors or omissions, or for damages resulting from the use of the information contained herein.

BEYOND THE FLESH: THE ETHICS OF ENHANCEMENT

First edition. November 24, 2024.

ISBN: 979-8230395164

Written by joseph demegillo.

Table of Contents

"In seeking to improve ourselves, we may be altering the very essence of what makes us human; yet, in that alteration, do we lose our humanity—or do we find it anew?" – J. T. Demegillo

Introduction

As humanity steps boldly into the 21st century, we find ourselves on the threshold of a profound technological transformation. What was once the realm of speculative fiction has now become a burgeoning reality. The rapid advancements in biotechnology, neuroengineering, and artificial intelligence are reshaping the contours of human existence, forcing us to confront fundamental questions about our identity and purpose. Beyond the Flesh: The Ethics of Enhancement is a journey into these uncharted waters, examining the exhilarating potential and ethical complexities of a future where the boundaries of human nature are no longer immutable.

For millennia, the human story has been one of aspiration—an unyielding drive to transcend the limitations imposed by our biology. From the rudimentary practices of ancient medicine to the cutting-edge innovations of genetic engineering, our desire to enhance our abilities and extend our lives has been a constant force propelling us forward. But today, as we wield tools capable of altering not only our bodies but also our consciousness, we must grapple with questions that strike at the very core of our humanity. What does it mean to be human in an age where nature itself can be rewritten? How do we navigate the moral landscape of a world where enhancement may redefine the essence of who we are?

This book seeks to illuminate both the promise and the peril of human enhancement technologies. On one hand, these innovations offer unprecedented opportunities to alleviate suffering, expand cognitive capacities, and extend lifespans. On the other hand, they present formidable ethical dilemmas: Who will have access to these advancements? Will they deepen societal inequalities or erode fundamental human values? And what will become of those who choose—or are unable—to embrace them? As these technologies blur the lines between human and machine, between natural and artificial, we are compelled to reconsider our collective identity and purpose.

Beyond the Flesh challenges readers to confront these urgent questions with both intellectual rigor and moral sensitivity. It explores the delicate balance between the pursuit of progress and the preservation of dignity, urging us to reflect on the kind of future we wish to create. As the power to reshape our physical and mental capacities becomes increasingly accessible, we must ask: Will this pursuit unite us in shared progress, or fracture us into a world of profound division? The answers lie not in technology alone, but in the values we choose to uphold. This is a time for introspection and dialogue—a moment to define what we stand for as a species standing on the precipice of transformation. Our choices today will echo far into the future, shaping not just our bodies and minds but the very fabric of human existence.

I invite you to approach this book with curiosity, logic, and an unwavering commitment to ethical inquiry. The questions posed here are not merely academic—they are a call to action. Challenge your assumptions, wrestle with uncertainty, and engage deeply with the dilemmas presented. Together, we can envision a future that is not only transformative but also just and compassionate.

Acknowledgments

To those who dare to challenge the status quo, to the scholars, visionaries, and creators who illuminate the uncharted realms of human potential. Your work inspires us to confront the complexities of progress with courage and critical thought.

To my family, whose unwavering belief in me provided the strength to undertake this journey. Your patience and encouragement have been my foundation, allowing me the space to explore these ideas with determination and focus.

To the academic pioneers like Nick Bostrom, Francis Fukuyama, Jennifer Doudna, and Emmanuelle Charpentier, whose groundbreaking insights into ethics, human identity, and biotechnology have profoundly shaped this work. Your contributions remind us that progress demands not just knowledge, but the wisdom to wield it responsibly.

To my friends and colleagues, whose thoughtful discussions, questions, and perspectives enriched these pages. You have reminded me that innovation flourishes not in isolation, but in the collective exchange of ideas that challenge and inspire.

To the readers who pick up this book, may it spark thoughtful reflection on the paths we choose to follow. Let this work serve as a reminder that the heart of human progress lies not solely in technological achievement, but in our shared commitment to justice, equity, and the preservation of our humanity.

This book is a product of the collective endeavor of thinkers, dreamers, and doers. To all who have contributed directly or indirectly, thank you. May we continue to strive for a future where innovation and ethics walk hand in hand, guiding humanity toward a horizon shaped by compassion, integrity, and shared purpose.

Part I: From Evolution to Revolution

Chapter 1: The Spark of Ingenuity

The story of human advancement begins not with great civilizations or towering monuments but in the quiet persistence of survival. In the dim glow of ancient fires, humanity's earliest ancestors embarked on a journey that would come to define their species—a relentless quest to transcend the limits imposed by nature. These moments, humble as they seem, laid the foundation for what would later be recognized as the human capacity for ingenuity. Millennia ago, early humans began grinding herbs into paste, applying these rudimentary concoctions to wounds with no formal understanding of medicine or biology. Yet, these primitive actions were far more than mere survival tactics. They represented a deliberate attempt to alter outcomes, to manipulate the natural world in ways no other species had before. It was not only the act itself but the mindset behind it—a nascent form of problem-solving and curiosity—that marked the beginning of humanity's exceptional trajectory.

The earliest evidence of human ingenuity can be traced to the development of tools and techniques that enhanced survival. Archeological findings indicate that early hominins used sharpened stones to cut meat or break open bones for marrow—a calorie-rich resource crucial for survival during periods of scarcity. Such tools were not merely functional; they symbolized the ability to observe, analyze, and adapt. The use of herbs for healing, while rudimentary, demonstrates early humans' capacity to experiment with their environment. Ethnobotanical studies reveal that many indigenous healing practices stem from observations of animals, such as primates consuming specific plants when ill. These early attempts to mimic nature marked the beginning of a larger journey—one in which humans sought to refine and perfect the processes they inherited from their surroundings. Fire, arguably one of the most transformative discoveries in human history, further exemplifies this ingenuity. Beyond its immediate benefits of warmth and protection, fire allowed humans to cook food, breaking down fibers and proteins to make nutrients more accessible. This innovation not only improved survival rates but also had far-reaching implications for human physiology, including the development of smaller guts and larger brains—a phenomenon known as the "expensive tissue hypothesis" (Aiello & Wheeler, 1995).

While the early stages of human ingenuity were driven largely by necessity, the trajectory soon shifted toward intentional self-improvement. This shift is evident in the development of more sophisticated tools and technologies. By the Upper Paleolithic period, approximately 40,000 years ago, humans were crafting specialized tools for hunting, fishing, and sewing. These tools were not only functional but also precise, reflecting a growing understanding of materials and mechanics. Moreover, symbolic expression began to emerge during this period, as seen in cave paintings, carvings, and ornaments. These artifacts suggest that humans were not only enhancing their physical capabilities but also exploring cognitive and cultural dimensions of existence. This development underscores the idea that the quest for enhancement was multifaceted, encompassing both practical and existential dimensions. The Neolithic Revolution, around 10,000 years ago, marked another critical juncture. The transition from hunter-gatherer societies to agricultural communities introduced new challenges and opportunities for ingenuity. Domestication of plants and animals required extensive knowledge of biology and environmental conditions. Irrigation systems, crop rotation, and selective breeding exemplify how humans began to manipulate nature on an unprecedented scale. These advancements not only ensured food security but also enabled the growth of complex societies, laying the groundwork for further innovation.

Chapter 2
Ancient Remedies, Modern Aspirations

Humanity's enduring quest to transcend its natural limits has shaped the development of medicine, biotechnology, and ethics throughout history. From the earliest herbal remedies to cutting-edge genetic engineering, this pursuit has been driven by the desire not only to cure disease but to enhance human capability. This chapter examines the evolution of these aspirations, from ancient healing practices to modern biotechnological breakthroughs, highlighting the intersection of cultural, technological, and ethical considerations. By integrating academic perspectives from history, medicine, philosophy, and bioethics, we aim to understand how humanity's desire for self-improvement has transformed over millennia.

Ancient healing practices were deeply intertwined with spiritual and philosophical beliefs, laying the groundwork for modern medicine. In the classical world, Greek medicine became a foundational model for understanding health, emphasizing balance within the human body. Hippocrates (circa 460–370 BCE), often regarded as the father of medicine, argued that disease was not caused by divine punishment but by natural factors, and that healing should involve restoring balance to the body's humors (Lloyd, 1978). His theory of the four humors—blood, phlegm, yellow bile, and black bile—became central to medical thought for centuries and influenced later medical systems, such as the Roman and Islamic medical traditions. The Greek concept of the "holistic" approach to health, which was later echoed by the Hippocratic Oath, laid the foundation for the biopsychosocial model of health, recognizing the interconnection between physical health, psychological well-being, and social factors (Engel, 1977). This was also reflected in other ancient medical systems, such as Traditional Chinese Medicine (TCM). In TCM, the concept of Qi (⟡), the vital life force that flows through the body, underscores the belief that health results from the proper balance of this energy. Imbalances in Qi are seen as the root cause of disease, and treatments such as acupuncture, herbal remedies, and Tai Chi aim to restore harmony within the body (Maciocia, 2005). Similarly, Indigenous medicine systems worldwide, such as those practiced by Native American, African, and Aboriginal Australian cultures, relied heavily on herbal remedies and spiritual healing. These systems emphasized the interconnectedness of nature and human beings and reflected a profound understanding of the body's relationship to the environment (Zoller & Duvall, 2008). These early practices, though not grounded in the scientific methodologies of today, demonstrated an acute awareness of the importance of balance and holistic approaches to health, which would influence later medical thought.

The Industrial Revolution (18th–19th centuries) dramatically shifted the focus of human enhancement. Whereas ancient practices sought to restore balance or cure disease, industrialization introduced technologies that focused on restoring lost functions. The growth of mechanized industries, coupled with advancements in scientific understanding, led to an era where corrective devices, pharmaceuticals, and medical instruments became central to the restoration of lost or impaired functions. One of the earliest examples of industrial-era restorative technology was the development of eyeglasses. Initially used for vision correction, eyeglasses extended human capability by restoring the ability to see clearly, allowing individuals with poor eyesight to engage fully in daily activities (Borelli et al., 2012). Prosthetics similarly became a symbol of human resilience, as devices to replace lost limbs began to evolve from rudimentary wooden structures to more advanced forms. The development of more functional prosthetics was catalyzed by advancements in materials science and biomechanics, notably in the 20th century, contributing to improved mobility and quality of life for amputees (Hunsaker et al., 2011). Vaccination, emerging in the 19th century through the work of Edward Jenner, marked another milestone in the restorative aspect of medicine. By preventing the spread of diseases such as smallpox, vaccines not only saved lives but also protected communities from devastating pandemics, thus reshaping global public health (Riedel, 2005). This focus on prevention marked a shift from curing diseases to averting them, heralding the rise of public health systems aimed at improving and restoring health on a global scale.

As the 20th century unfolded, the focus of human enhancement expanded beyond mere restoration. The field of biotechnology, spurred by the discovery of the structure of DNA in 1953 by Watson and Crick, opened new possibilities for human enhancement at the genetic level (Watson & Crick, 1953). Genetic engineering, the process of modifying an organism's DNA, initially focused on curing genetic disorders such as cystic fibrosis and hemophilia. However, over time, it raised new questions about the potential for "enhancing" the human genome itself. The ethical implications of genetic engineering were widely debated, particularly with the advent of technologies such as CRISPR-Cas9, which allowed for precise gene editing. While these advancements hold promise for eradicating hereditary diseases, they also pose risks associated with unintended genetic mutations and the potential creation of genetic "designer babies" (Baylis, 2019). The ability to edit genes and enhance human traits—ranging from physical characteristics like strength and intelligence to resistance to disease—raises critical ethical questions about consent, inequality, and the commodification of human life (Sandel, 2007). As such, biotechnology has become both a tool for healing and a source of ethical controversy. In parallel, advancements in neuroprosthetics, including devices like cochlear implants and deep brain stimulation (DBS), have made it possible to restore or enhance cognitive and sensory functions. Cochlear implants, for instance, allow those with severe hearing loss to regain auditory perception, while DBS has shown promise in treating neurological disorders such as Parkinson's disease (Baker et al., 2018). These technologies represent the next frontier in human enhancement, where the lines between biological and artificial intelligence begin to blur. Similarly, the development of brain-computer interfaces (BCIs), which allow direct communication between the brain and external devices, points to the potential for enhancing cognitive and motor capabilities in individuals with disabilities, while also raising questions about the possible enhancements for healthy individuals (Lebedev & Nicolelis, 2006). As these technologies evolve, they offer the potential not only for restoration but also for augmentation, enabling humans to surpass their biological limitations.

As biotechnologies continue to evolve, they bring with them significant ethical challenges that demand careful consideration. A major concern is the potential for inequality in access to enhancement technologies. As these technologies become more sophisticated and expensive, there is a risk that only certain segments of society will benefit, exacerbating existing inequalities (Greenfield, 2011). The prospect of a "genetic divide" between the enhanced and the unenhanced raises fundamental questions about fairness, justice, and the future of social structures. Moreover, as humanity increasingly embraces the potential for enhancement, we must also consider the philosophical implications of altering the human condition. What does it mean to be human when our physical and cognitive capacities are augmented by technology? Philosophers such as Nick Bostrom (2008) have argued that enhancing human capabilities could lead to unintended consequences, including the loss of essential aspects of humanity, such as vulnerability, imperfection, and empathy. This debate highlights the tension between the potential for improvement and the preservation of human dignity.

Chapter 3

Beyond Restoration - The Birth of Revolution

The 20th century heralded a paradigm shift in human existence, as the accelerating pace of technological advancements began to challenge humanity's age-old understanding of its limitations. As scientific breakthroughs unfolded across fields such as biotechnology, cognitive science, and nanotechnology, the lines between the natural and the enhanced, between evolution and intentional modification, began to blur. Once considered the stuff of science fiction, these advancements rapidly became the cornerstone of a new era—one in which humans no longer simply adapted to their environment but began to shape their biological and cognitive landscapes actively. In this chapter, we explore the profound implications of these developments, examining the revolutionary forces that are redefining human nature and identity.

Biotechnology has undergone significant advancements over the last century, evolving from rudimentary techniques in agriculture and medicine to complex tools capable of altering the very essence of life. The discovery of the double helix structure of DNA in the 1950s paved the way for a deeper understanding of genetics, and with it, the birth of genetic engineering. Early biotechnological applications, such as the creation of recombinant DNA and genetically modified organisms (GMOs), laid the groundwork for more ambitious endeavors in the realm of genetic modification and enhancement. By the late 20th century, genetically engineered bacteria had been employed to produce insulin, a breakthrough that revolutionized the treatment of diabetes. However, it was the advent of precise gene-editing techniques, such as CRISPR-Cas9, that sparked the most transformative shift. Developed in the early 21st century, CRISPR-Cas9 has become one of the most significant tools in genetic engineering. By enabling the precise editing of genetic material, CRISPR has opened up possibilities once deemed unimaginable. Diseases rooted in genetic mutations, such as sickle cell anemia and cystic fibrosis, could potentially be eradicated at the genetic level. Furthermore, scientists began to entertain the possibility of using genetic modification for human enhancement—designing individuals with desirable traits such as heightened intelligence, physical endurance, and resistance to disease. The ethical implications of such possibilities are profound, and scholars such as Julian Savulescu (2001) have raised concerns about the emergence of a "genetic underclass," where only the wealthy have access to genetic enhancements, thereby exacerbating existing social inequalities. The very idea of genetic enhancement challenges traditional notions of human nature and evolution. Historically, human evolution was seen as a slow, natural process shaped by random mutations and natural selection. With the advent of genetic engineering, however, humans have gained the ability to directly alter their genetic code. This shift raises fundamental questions about the ethics of such modifications: who decides which traits are desirable, and should genetic enhancement be limited to curing diseases or expanded to include the enhancement of non-pathological traits? As biotechnology continues to evolve, so too will these ethical debates, with far-reaching implications for future generations.

Parallel to the rise of biotechnology, the fields of cognitive science and neuroengineering began to emerge as areas of intense research. With advancements in neuroscience and psychology, scientists were gaining a deeper understanding of the human brain and its capacity for learning, memory, and problem-solving. As our understanding of cognition deepened, it became increasingly apparent that the limitations of human intelligence were not necessarily immutable. Cognitive enhancement refers to the use of various interventions—ranging from pharmaceuticals to brain-computer interfaces—to improve cognitive functions such as memory, attention, and decision-making. One of the most notable advances in this area has been the development of nootropics, or "smart drugs," which are substances designed to improve mental performance. These substances, which include compounds such as modafinil and racetams, have gained popularity in both academic and professional circles as ways to enhance cognitive abilities, particularly in high-stakes environments such as business and academia. While some studies suggest that nootropics may have cognitive benefits, others have raised concerns about their long-term effects and the potential for misuse in non-medical contexts (Bostrom & Sandberg, 2009). In addition to pharmacological interventions, the advent of brain-computer interfaces (BCIs) has opened new possibilities for enhancing human cognition. BCIs allow for direct communication between the brain and external devices, enabling individuals to control computers, prosthetics, and even exoskeletons with their thoughts.

The potential applications of BCIs are vast, ranging from restoring lost sensory functions to enabling enhanced mental capabilities such as memory augmentation or direct neural interfacing with artificial intelligence. Research in this area has shown that BCIs can improve motor function in individuals with paralysis, and ongoing developments are focused on creating more seamless and efficient interfaces (Lebedev & Nicolelis, 2006). The potential for cognitive enhancement raises significant ethical and philosophical questions. At the core of these debates is the issue of access: if cognitive enhancements become widely available, will they exacerbate social inequalities, with only the privileged having access to superior mental abilities? In a qworld where cognitive performance is increasingly linked to economic success, will individuals be under increasing pressure to enhance their brains, leading to the commodification of human cognition? The prospect of cognitive enhancement also raises questions about the authenticity of enhanced mental processes—if individuals can modify their cognition, what becomes of their sense of self, and how does this affect our understanding of human identity?

Nanotechnology, the manipulation of matter on an atomic or molecular scale, offers profound possibilities for transforming human health and longevity. In the early 21st century, the promise of nanotechnology extended beyond industrial and material applications to the realm of medicine.

BEYOND THE FLESH: THE ETHICS OF ENHANCEMENT

The potential for nanobots—microscopic robots capable of operating at the cellular level—has captivated researchers and visionaries alike. These nanobots could be designed to perform medical tasks such as repairing damaged tissues, delivering drugs directly to cancer cells, or even reversing the aging process by repairing cellular damage. One of the most exciting prospects of nanotechnology lies in its potential to revolutionize the treatment of diseases. Traditional medical interventions often involve systemic treatments, which can have significant side effects due to their lack of precision. Nanobots, by contrast, could target specific cells or tissues, delivering highly targeted treatments with minimal collateral damage. For instance, nanobots could deliver chemotherapy drugs directly to cancerous cells, avoiding the healthy cells that are often affected by traditional treatments. Similarly, nanobots could be employed to repair tissues at the cellular level, potentially restoring organs that have been damaged by injury or disease (Mayer, 2013). Beyond medical applications, nanotechnology also holds promise for extending human lifespan. As humans age, the cells in their bodies undergo damage that accumulates over time, leading to the decline of bodily functions.

Nanotechnology offers the possibility of reversing this damage by repairing cells at the molecular level. Some researchers have proposed that, by using nanobots to repair the cellular damage associated with aging, humans could potentially extend their lifespans indefinitely (Joyce et al., 2005). While these ideas remain speculative, the rapid pace of advancements in nanotechnology suggests that such possibilities may not be as far-fetched as they once seemed.

However, the potential of nanotechnology to transform human biology also raises a host of ethical and social concerns. The ability to manipulate biological systems at such a fundamental level could lead to profound shifts in human identity and societal structures. If nanotechnology enables the repair of damaged organs or the extension of life, how will these advances be distributed across society? Will they be available to everyone, or will only the wealthy have access to these life-saving technologies? Furthermore, as nanotechnology becomes more integrated into human biology, the distinction between natural and artificial may become increasingly difficult to draw. What will it mean to be human in a world where biological enhancements are commonplace?

Chapter 4
The Human-Machine Convergence

The merging of humans and machines marks a turning point in our history. We're entering an era where technology not only supports us but becomes a part of us. This chapter explores how cybernetic augmentation—using advanced technology to enhance the human body and mind—is reshaping what it means to be human. From brain implants that connect thoughts to computers to wearable devices evolving into embedded systems, the line between humans and machines is becoming harder to define. But as these technologies develop, so do the ethical, philosophical, and social questions they raise.

Human-machine integration isn't new. For centuries, we've used tools and technologies to improve our lives. What's different now is how closely machines are merging with us. Instead of tools we hold or wear, we're moving toward devices that become a permanent part of our bodies. One area leading this change is neural augmentation—technologies that link the human brain with machines. For example, Elon Musk's Neuralink is working on brain implants that let people control devices with their thoughts. Early uses are focused on helping people with disabilities, like restoring movement for those who are paralyzed. But in the future, these brain-machine interfaces could improve our memory, boost intelligence, or let us communicate faster than ever before. Wearable technologies like smart watches and augmented reality glasses are already enhancing how we interact with the world. These devices track our health, connect us to digital spaces, and even help us see or hear better. Over time, wearables may become embedded technologies, built into our bodies. For example, tiny devices under the skin could monitor our health continuously or give us superhuman senses, like seeing infrared light or hearing sounds outside normal ranges.

As technologies become more advanced, they challenge basic ideas about what it means to be human. If you have a brain implant that makes you smarter, are you still the same person? If machines enhance our physical abilities or senses, are we crossing a line into something new—something beyond human? These questions are part of a growing field called post-humanism, which looks at how technology might change human nature itself. Thinkers like Francis Fukuyama worry that such changes could divide society. If some people have access to expensive enhancements and others don't, will we create a new class of "superhumans" while leaving others behind? Philosophers have long debated what makes us human. For example, Jean-Paul Sartre argued that being human means making choices and defining ourselves through our actions. But if machines take over parts of our thinking or acting, do we lose some of that freedom? Enhancements might give us more abilities, but they could also make us more dependent on technology, blurring the boundaries of our individuality.

The exciting possibilities of human enhancement come with serious ethical challenges. One big issue is access—who gets to use these technologies? If enhancements are expensive, only the wealthy might afford them, creating an even larger gap between rich and poor. Another concern is pressure to enhance. If enhancements become normal, people might feel forced to use them just to keep up at work, school, or in society. Imagine a world where employers prefer workers with brain implants or students with augmented memory. This could lead to a loss of choice—people might enhance themselves not because they want to, but because they feel they have to. There's also the question of safety and regulation. Who makes sure these technologies are safe? What if something goes wrong with a brain implant, or an embedded device gets hacked? Governments and scientists will need to work together to create rules that protect people while still allowing innovation. As humans and machines merge, the way we live, think, and interact with the world will change in ways we can barely imagine. Cybernetic enhancements could lead to incredible breakthroughs, from curing diseases to expanding human abilities beyond natural limits. But they also force us to think deeply about what kind of future we want. Will we embrace a world where technology is part of us, or will we draw the line to preserve our human nature? As we navigate this convergence, we must ensure that these advancements benefit everyone and protect the core values that make us human: freedom, equality, and dignity.

Chapter 5
Redefining Evolution

The concept of evolution is foundational to our understanding of life. Traditionally, evolution has been a slow, natural process shaped by environmental pressures and genetic mutations. However, the 21st century has introduced a new dimension to this process: human-driven evolution. Unlike its natural counterpart, this form of evolution does not wait for the passage of millennia but occurs at an unprecedented pace, driven by breakthroughs in science and technology. Genetic engineering, biotechnology, artificial intelligence, and nanotechnology are all converging to give humanity control over its evolutionary trajectory. In this chapter, we explore how these advancements redefine what it means to evolve. We examine the implications of this shift, asking profound questions about identity, survival, and responsibility. As we push the boundaries of nature, we must also confront the challenges and ethical dilemmas that arise from such profound power. Are we prepared for the world we are creating? And how will this redefinition of evolution impact the future of humanity?

For centuries, Charles Darwin's theory of natural selection has been the cornerstone of evolutionary biology. The idea that organisms adapt to their environment over time through random genetic mutations and survival pressures has explained the diversity of life on Earth. But the advent of designer evolution—the deliberate manipulation of genetic material to achieve desired outcomes—challenges these principles. The tools of designer evolution, such as CRISPR-Cas9, have revolutionized genetic engineering. With precision editing, scientists can now modify DNA to eliminate diseases, enhance physical or cognitive traits, and even create entirely new forms of life. Unlike the randomness of natural selection, designer evolution operates with intentionality. It allows humanity to bypass the slow mechanisms of nature and shape evolution according to its needs and desires. However, this shift raises significant questions. If evolution is no longer governed by nature but by human intention, who decides what traits are worth enhancing? Furthermore, does this newfound control over our biology risk erasing the diversity that natural evolution has fostered over billions of years?

The concept of "survival of the fittest" is being replaced by "survival of the enhanced." The enhancement revolution, fueled by advancements in biotechnology and artificial intelligence, enables individuals to transcend their biological limitations. Physical strength, cognitive abilities, and even emotional resilience can now be augmented. One area of profound impact is gene therapy, which holds the potential to cure genetic disorders and prevent hereditary diseases. For example, clinical trials using CRISPR have shown promise in treating conditions like sickle cell anemia and muscular dystrophy. But beyond therapeutic uses, genetic editing also opens the door to enhancements—modifications aimed not at treating illness but at improving human capabilities. Another transformative field is bionics and prosthetics. Advanced prosthetic limbs integrated with neural interfaces allow individuals to regain or surpass their original physical capabilities. Similarly, wearable or implantable devices that monitor and regulate physiological functions blur the line between human and machine. These technologies redefine not only how we interact with the world but also how we perceive ourselves. The enhancement revolution also extends to cognitive abilities. Brain-computer interfaces (BCIs), like those developed by Neuralink, promise to expand memory, boost intelligence, and create seamless communication between humans and machines. As these technologies become more sophisticated, they challenge the traditional boundaries of human potential.

With great power comes great responsibility. The ability to reshape evolution raises ethical questions that humanity has never faced before. One of the most pressing issues is equity. If enhancements are expensive and accessible only to the wealthy, they could exacerbate existing inequalities, creating a world divided into "enhanced" and "unenhanced" populations. Such disparities could lead to a form of biological elitism, where the enhanced have advantages in health, intelligence, and physical abilities, further widening social and economic gaps. Another ethical dilemma concerns consent and autonomy. In the case of genetic modifications performed on embryos, future individuals have no say in the changes made to their DNA. This raises questions about the rights of individuals to determine their genetic makeup and whether such decisions should be left to parents, scientists, or policymakers. Additionally, the prospect of unintended consequences looms large. The complexity of biological systems means that even small genetic changes can have unpredictable effects. For example, editing a gene to enhance intelligence might inadvertently increase susceptibility to mental health disorders. The long-term impacts of such modifications are still unknown, making caution essential as we venture into this uncharted territory.

The ability to alter our biology challenges fundamental notions of identity. Historically, our understanding of what it means to be human has been rooted in our shared vulnerabilities, limitations, and mortality. Technologies that enable us to transcend these limitations force us to rethink these definitions. For example, if a person with extensive genetic enhancements or bionic implants can outperform an unenhanced individual in nearly every way, are they still considered human? Philosophers in the field of posthumanism argue that humanity may evolve into something entirely new—a species that blends biological and artificial elements seamlessly. This redefinition of identity also extends to relationships and social structures. As individuals gain the ability to enhance themselves, societal norms and values may shift. Will traditional notions of equality, fairness, and meritocracy hold up in a world where enhancement is the norm? Furthermore, the rise of cognitive enhancements raises questions about individuality. If thoughts, memories, and emotions can be manipulated or shared through brain-computer interfaces, what happens to personal identity? Will individuals lose their sense of self as their minds become intertwined with technology?

As we navigate this era of human-driven evolution, preparation is essential. Scientists, policymakers, and society at large must work together to ensure that these advancements are used responsibly and equitably. One crucial step is the establishment of global guidelines and regulations. International collaboration is necessary to prevent the misuse of technologies like genetic editing and to ensure that their benefits are distributed fairly. Ethical frameworks must prioritize transparency, safety, and inclusivity. Education will also play a vital role. As technologies reshape the job market, healthcare, and daily life, individuals must be equipped with the knowledge and skills to adapt. Public awareness campaigns can help demystify complex topics like genetic engineering and artificial intelligence, fostering informed discussions about their implications. Finally, fostering a culture of ethical innovation is key. Scientists and technologists must prioritize the well-being of humanity over profit or prestige. By embedding ethical considerations into the design and implementation of new technologies, we can create a future that reflects our highest values.

The redefinition of evolution represents both a profound opportunity and a significant challenge. For the first time in history, humanity holds the tools to shape its own destiny, transcending the limitations imposed by nature. But with this power comes the responsibility to act wisely. As we stand on the brink of this new chapter, we must ask ourselves: what kind of future do we want to create? Will we use these advancements to build a more equitable and inclusive world, or will we allow them to deepen divisions and inequalities? Will we respect the delicate balance of nature, or will we push forward without considering the consequences? Redefining evolution is not just about enhancing our biology; it is about reimagining what it means to be human. It challenges us to think deeply about our values, priorities, and aspirations. The choices we make today will shape the trajectory of our species for generations to come.

32

Part II: Ethics at the Edge of Perfection

Chapter 6: The Ethics of Transcendence—Redefining Human Boundaries

The pursuit of human transcendence—whether through biological, cognitive, or cybernetic enhancements—has become one of the most profound and contentious ethical dilemmas of our age. As we approach a future where human boundaries are increasingly malleable, the very definition of what it means to be human is being challenged. The question of whether we should enhance ourselves, transcend our evolutionary limits, or remain within the natural constraints of our species is a complex one, involving both profound philosophical inquiry and practical ethical concerns. This chapter will explore the ethics surrounding human transcendence by examining the nature of human limits, the role of enhancement technologies in redefining our species, and the moral implications of tampering with our own biological and cognitive foundations.

Historically, the idea of human enhancement has been guided by a tension between the perceived potential of humanity and the limitations imposed by nature. Natural law theory, which asserts that there are inherent moral principles and rights embedded in human nature, has long served as a foundation for debates on human limits. In this view, human beings are governed by a natural order that is either divinely ordained or rooted in human reason. From the perspective of natural law, the body, mind, and the natural world are seen as interrelated and defined by an immutable set of moral laws. The very concept of human nature—what it means to be human—has been traditionally understood within this framework. The most influential proponent of natural law in Western thought, Thomas Aquinas, argued that human beings should seek to align their actions with the divine will as revealed through nature. He posited that the purpose of human life is to fulfill the potential inherent in human nature, a process which requires adhering to a set of moral principles that align with divine law. Enhancing or altering this nature, according to Aquinas, could be seen as an affront to God's plan. If human beings are meant to exist in a certain way—biologically and cognitively—then any attempt to improve upon that design may be viewed as an act of hubris, an attempt to exceed the natural boundaries established by divine creation (Aquinas, T. Summa Theologica).

This idea has profound implications for the ethical evaluation of enhancement technologies. From gene editing to cognitive implants, enhancement technologies represent the ability to transcend our natural limitations. But in doing so, we face a core ethical dilemma: is it morally justifiable to alter the human body and mind to a state of "perfection" that exceeds the capacities envisioned by natural law? If we tamper with human nature, are we undermining the essence of what it means to be human, or are we fulfilling our natural duty to improve ourselves, to evolve in accordance with reason? Aquinas' natural law theory does not prohibit human progress or the use of reason to develop tools and technologies that improve human life. However, it suggests that any such advancements must not violate the natural order, which includes respecting human dignity, autonomy, and the intrinsic value of the human person. The use of enhancement technologies must therefore be evaluated not only in terms of their potential benefits but also with regard to their alignment with natural law, which prioritizes human flourishing within the bounds of divinely designed limits (Aquinas, T., On Law, Morality, and Politics).

As humanity seeks to push the boundaries of biology and cognition, Immanuel Kant's philosophy provides a critical framework for considering the ethical implications of human enhancement. Kant emphasized the intrinsic value of human autonomy, arguing that every individual possesses inherent dignity and moral worth. Human beings, according to Kant, are not merely objects to be manipulated or perfected but are ends in themselves, deserving of respect and freedom. This principle of autonomy places significant moral weight on the decisions individuals make about their own lives and bodies (Kant, I. Groundwork of the Metaphysics of Morals). In the context of human enhancement, the ethical challenge is whether we can maintain the dignity and autonomy of the individual as we modify their very nature. Enhancements, particularly those that involve altering cognition or biology at a deep level, may threaten this autonomy. If enhancements are imposed from the outside, particularly by powerful institutions, corporations, or even the state, the individual's capacity for self-determination may be compromised. There is a real risk that enhancements could become a tool of social control, where individuals are engineered to conform to societal norms or expectations, rather than being allowed to develop their unique potential. Moreover, if enhancements are designed to perfect human beings, then the very notion of what it means to be human is challenged.

By attempting to remove human imperfection, we might unintentionally reduce human beings to mere projects of technological design, beings created not through natural processes but through the manipulation of genetic code or neural connections. This undermines the Kantian notion of human beings as free moral agents, capable of defining their own identity and values. In Kant's view, the essence of human dignity lies in the capacity for moral choice and the ability to pursue one's own happiness within the bounds of moral law. Enhancement technologies that undermine the autonomy of individuals, whether through genetic manipulation or cognitive engineering, could threaten this capacity for self-determination. Thus, a key ethical concern in the debate over human enhancement is whether the pursuit of perfection compromises human autonomy by reducing individuals to engineered products, rather than beings with intrinsic value and moral agency (Kant, I. Critique of Practical Reason).

A critical part of the ethical conversation surrounding human enhancement involves theological considerations about human creation and the relationship between humanity and God. The idea of humanity as created in the image of God, or imago Dei, is a foundational concept in many religious traditions, particularly in Christianity. According to this view, human beings are not only natural creatures but also spiritual beings imbued with inherent dignity and purpose by God (Genesis 1:26-27). The question that arises when considering human enhancement is whether altering human nature through technological means is an affront to God's sovereignty. If God created humanity in a particular way, and if human beings are created in His image, can we justify changing our own biology or cognition? Some religious perspectives argue that to enhance human beings is to challenge the divine order, as it implies that God's creation is imperfect and requires correction or improvement.

From this perspective, human enhancement represents a form of prideful disobedience—a failure to recognize the sanctity of God's plan (Pope John Paul II, Evangelium Vitae). Alternatively, there are theological viewpoints that assert that it is within humanity's divine mandate to exercise dominion over creation. Genesis 1:28 instructs humanity to "fill the earth and subdue it," which some interpret as a call to develop and transform the world, including human nature, to fulfill our divine potential. From this perspective, enhancement technologies are not seen as a challenge to divine sovereignty but rather as an expression of human creativity and responsibility in carrying out God's will. If we possess the knowledge and tools to improve human life and transcend our limitations, then it may be our duty to do so in a way that maximizes human flourishing (Gifford, P. Theology and Technology). However, this argument raises further ethical questions: If we are to exercise dominion over ourselves, how far should we go in reshaping our biology and cognition? Is there a limit to our power over creation, or can we continue to modify our bodies and minds without restriction? These questions are particularly urgent as we move closer to a reality where human enhancement technologies have the potential to radically alter the very essence of human existence. Theologically, the ethics of enhancement technologies can be framed within the context of stewardship—the idea that humanity has a moral obligation to care for and nurture the world and its creatures, including themselves. This notion suggests that human enhancement should be pursued with caution and responsibility, ensuring that any changes to human nature are made with a deep respect for the sanctity of life, the dignity of individuals, and the ethical implications of tampering with the divine design (McFague, S. The Body of God).

As we stand on the threshold of unprecedented technological advancements, the ethical dilemmas surrounding human enhancement continue to grow more complex. Can we justify the pursuit of human transcendence through technology, or does it represent an ethical overreach? The tension between the desire to transcend our natural limitations and the responsibility to respect the moral and spiritual laws that govern our existence is not easily resolved. On one hand, the potential benefits of human enhancement are vast. By overcoming biological limitations, enhancing cognitive capacities, and extending human lifespan, we could usher in an era of unparalleled human flourishing. On the other hand, the risks associated with enhancement—ranging from unintended societal consequences to the erosion of individual autonomy—are equally significant. The ethics of enhancement technologies thus require careful consideration, balancing the potential for progress with the need to safeguard human dignity, autonomy, and the integrity of the natural world. At the heart of the ethical conversation about human transcendence is the question of what it means to be human. Is our humanity defined by our biological limitations, or can we transcend those boundaries and still remain authentically human? In the quest for perfection, are we losing the very qualities that make us human—our vulnerability, our imperfections, our capacity for growth and change? Ultimately, the ethical implications of human enhancement challenge us to reconsider the very nature of human existence. To transcend our limits is to confront the tension between aspiration and identity, between the pursuit of perfection and the acceptance of imperfection. Whether through enhancing our bodies or minds, or even merging with machines, the choices we make today will shape the future of what it means to be human. In considering the ethical dimensions of these choices, we must grapple with the values that define us—not only as individuals but as a species.

One of the most compelling ethical concerns about human enhancement is the risk of dehumanization. As enhancement technologies become more accessible, we may face the growing temptation to treat human beings as objects to be perfected or optimized. The increasing ability to design human beings according to idealized standards—whether in terms of physical beauty, intelligence, or emotional resilience—poses a threat to the intrinsic worth of individuals. The individual may become less of a unique person with inherent value and more of a product to be fine-tuned according to external expectations or societal pressures. The fear of dehumanization can be traced to the philosophical work of Karl Marx, who warned about the dangers of reducing human beings to mere commodities in a technological society. Marx's critique of capitalism highlighted how technology, rather than serving humanity, could transform people into tools, controlled and manipulated for the benefit of economic systems rather than individual autonomy (Marx, K. Economic and Philosophic Manuscripts of 1844). In this regard, enhancement technologies may unintentionally shift the focus from individual dignity to a societal demand for uniformity, where every person is expected to meet the same enhanced standard. Moreover, the risk of class divisions based on access to enhancement technologies presents a serious ethical challenge. If only the wealthy or powerful are able to afford such enhancements, we may face a future of biological inequality, where those who are "perfected" are granted greater opportunities, while those who are not enhanced are relegated to a lower social status. The potential for a genetic divide between enhanced and non-enhanced individuals raises questions about social justice and equality. As biotechnologies, cognitive implants, and other enhancements become more widespread, ensuring that these advancements do not deepen societal divides becomes a central ethical responsibility (Sandel, M. J. The Case Against Perfection).

As we venture into an era of rapid scientific and technological development, the responsibility for the ethical deployment of enhancement technologies cannot be ignored. Scientists and ethicists alike must engage in continuous reflection about the implications of their work on society at large.

BEYOND THE FLESH: THE ETHICS OF ENHANCEMENT

The drive for progress must be tempered with a sense of responsibility—responsibility not just for the immediate benefits of technology, but for its long-term societal consequences. This responsibility extends to the safeguarding of individual rights, particularly freedom of choice, and the prevention of harm. Ethicists like Jürgen Habermas argue that scientific advancements must be aligned with democratic principles and respect for human autonomy (Habermas, J. The Future of Human Nature). Habermas highlights the potential dangers of genetic engineering and cognitive enhancement, warning that such technologies may infringe upon the autonomy of future generations by permanently altering their biological and cognitive makeup without their consent. In this sense, enhancement technologies not only challenge current moral frameworks but also raise concerns about the future moral agency of individuals who have yet to be born. The discussion surrounding informed consent is particularly important when considering the ethics of human enhancement. If a society chooses to adopt enhancement technologies, it must ensure that all individuals have the right to make informed decisions about whether to participate in such advancements. This includes understanding the risks, benefits, and potential consequences of undergoing enhancements. Informed consent must be a foundational ethical principle in the deployment of these technologies, ensuring that autonomy is respected and that individuals are not coerced or manipulated into enhancements they do not want (Glover, J. Choosing Children: Genes, Disability, and Design).

The conversation about human transcendence inevitably brings us to the concept of transhumanism—a philosophical and intellectual movement that advocates for the use of technology to enhance human physical and cognitive abilities. Transhumanists argue that by embracing enhancements, humanity can overcome its biological limitations and potentially achieve a post-human condition. In their view, human transcendence is not only possible but desirable, as it offers the chance to eliminate suffering, extend life, and achieve intellectual and emotional growth to unprecedented levels. However, transhumanism raises significant questions about identity and authenticity. If humans transform themselves into post-human beings, do they lose the essence of what it means to be human? Are we still human if we are no longer bound by biological limitations, if our memories and consciousness are uploaded into machines, or if our bodies are entirely replaced by artificial components? As the debate surrounding transhumanism continues to unfold, it is crucial to examine these questions from both an ethical and existential perspective (Bostrom, N. Transhumanist Values). As we navigate the ethical challenges of human enhancement, it is essential to develop a comprehensive ethical framework that can guide decision-making in the age of transcendence. This framework must address multiple dimensions, including the respect for individual rights, the prevention of harm, the safeguarding of social justice, and the preservation of human dignity. Ethics of care, as advocated by scholars such as Carol Gilligan, offers one potential framework for understanding how to navigate the personal and societal dimensions of enhancement technologies. The ethics of care emphasizes empathy, responsibility, and relational ethics, suggesting that we should focus on ensuring that technological advancements promote the well-being of all individuals, especially the most vulnerable (Gilligan, C. In a Different Voice). Another critical ethical lens is the virtue ethics of Aristotle, which asks not just about what actions are right but about what kinds of people we want to be. Virtue ethics suggests that the goal of human life is not simply to achieve perfection, but to develop virtues—qualities such as wisdom, courage, and compassion—that allow individuals to flourish within the natural world. From this perspective, enhancement technologies must be assessed not only by their ability to increase human capabilities but by their potential to nurture human virtues and contribute to a flourishing society (Aristotle, Nicomachean Ethics).

The ethics of human transcendence demand a careful balance between progress and preservation—between the desire to enhance human capabilities and the need to respect the fundamental dignity and autonomy of individuals. As we stand at the crossroads of unprecedented technological advancements, it is clear that the choices we make today will shape the trajectory of humanity's future. The pursuit of transcendence should not come at the cost of our core human values—our autonomy, dignity, and respect for the natural world. The ethical challenges of human enhancement remind us of the need for humility in the face of technological power. While we should embrace progress and seek to enhance human well-being, we must also be mindful of the risks involved in tampering with the very essence of what it means to be human. By grounding our pursuit of transcendence in ethical principles that respect human dignity, autonomy, and the natural order, we can ensure that the quest for human enhancement leads to a future that is not only technologically advanced but also morally just and socially responsible.

Chapter 7
The Price of Perfection— Access, Inequality, and Social Justice

John Rawls' Theory of Justice (1971) offers a critical lens through which to examine the ethical distribution of enhancement technologies. Rawls proposes a model of justice based on fairness, emphasizing the importance of equitable access to resources, particularly for the least advantaged members of society. His concept of the "veil of ignorance" urges us to design a society without knowledge of our own social position. This thought experiment challenges us to advocate for policies that would ensure fair access to advancements like human enhancement technologies, preventing a scenario where only the wealthy benefit. Rawls' difference principle posits that societal inequalities are justifiable only if they benefit the least advantaged. When applied to the issue of human enhancement, this principle suggests that access to such technologies should be distributed in a way that benefits all, especially those most likely to be excluded. If enhancement technologies become largely accessible only to the wealthy, they would violate this principle, deepening social disparities.

In Rawls' words:

"Justice is the first virtue of social institutions, as truth is of systems of thought." (Rawls, Theory of Justice)

This powerful assertion calls us to recognize the importance of fairness in the distribution of advancements that could shape the future of humanity. Rawls' framework suggests that policymakers should focus on creating opportunities for the most disadvantaged, ensuring that they have access to new technologies in a manner that promotes social equality.

Utilitarianism, a philosophy advanced by figures like Jeremy Bentham and John Stuart Mill, prioritizes the maximization of overall well-being. In the context of human enhancement, utilitarianism presents a challenging question: Can the pursuit of human perfection through technology be justified if it leads to an overall increase in societal happiness, even if some people are left behind? Peter Singer (1979) argues that human enhancement technologies, which improve cognitive function, reduce suffering from genetic diseases, and enhance productivity, could lead to a more prosperous society. However, the benefits of these technologies may not be distributed equally, exacerbating existing social inequalities. As critics such as Michael Sandel (2007) argue, the unequal distribution of enhancement technologies could create social divisions, making a utilitarian approach problematic.

Bentham, the founder of utilitarianism, writes:

"The greatest happiness of the greatest number is the foundation of morals and legislation."

This maxim emphasizes the ethical obligation to prioritize societal well-being. However, applying this principle to human enhancement raises complex questions about the trade-offs between overall happiness and individual equity. The core dilemma lies in balancing the utilitarian goal of maximizing societal well-being with the need for fairness and equality. If these technologies disproportionately benefit the wealthy, the overall societal good might be undermined by further marginalizing the disadvantaged.

Natural law theory, deeply rooted in the works of Aristotle and Thomas Aquinas, asserts that there are universal moral principles inherent in the natural world, accessible through human reason. Central to this philosophy is the concept of human equality, which holds that all individuals possess inherent dignity and worth, regardless of social or economic status. From a natural law perspective, the introduction of human enhancement technologies must be scrutinized for its potential to violate the principle of human equality. If these technologies become the preserve of the wealthy, it would not only exacerbate social inequalities but also undermine the fundamental value of human dignity. Enhancement technologies that create a divided society, where access is determined by wealth rather than equality, would be contrary to the very principles that natural law seeks to uphold. The German philosopher Immanuel Kant, in his Groundwork for the Metaphysics of Morals (1785), emphasized the intrinsic value of human beings:

"Humanity, whether in your own person or in the person of another, always at the same time as an end, never merely as a means."

This idea aligns with the belief that human dignity should not be commodified or diminished by the unequal distribution of enhancements. Enhancement technologies that only benefit a select few would violate this Kantian principle, as they reduce the vast majority of humanity to mere means to an end. The challenge, therefore, lies in whether the pursuit of human enhancement aligns with the natural law concept of human flourishing. Proponents of enhancement argue that such technologies can help individuals reach their fullest potential. However, critics caution that, in a society marked by unequal access to these technologies, we may lose sight of the value of natural human diversity and the unique abilities that each individual possesses.

Capitalism has driven much of the technological progress, including in the realm of human enhancement. However, the profit-driven nature of capitalism poses significant concerns for the equitable distribution of these advancements. The commercialization of enhancement technologies could lead to a situation where only the affluent have access to life-altering enhancements, further entrenching social inequality. The commodification of human enhancement could create a "genetic aristocracy," where wealthier individuals are able to afford superior capabilities while others remain disadvantaged. Critics like Sandel (2007) argue that the market-driven approach to human enhancement may reduce human beings to mere commodities to be enhanced and sold, undermining their inherent dignity.

Karl Marx, in his Critique of the Gotha Program (1875), warns about the dangers of capitalism exacerbating social inequalities:

"From each according to his ability, to each according to his needs."

This call for a more equitable distribution of resources resonates with the growing concern that the capitalist system may exploit human enhancement technologies to benefit the wealthy, leaving the poor further behind. From a policy perspective, it is crucial to regulate the distribution of enhancement technologies to prevent such disparities. Government intervention may be necessary to ensure that these advancements are available to all, not just those who can afford them. This could involve public healthcare initiatives, subsidies for enhancement technologies, or government-funded research to ensure that access is not solely determined by economic status.

Chapter 8

The Ethics of Autonomy—Choosing Our Own Evolution

In an era where the boundaries of human potential are increasingly defined by technological intervention, the concept of autonomy—particularly the autonomy to shape and redefine our biological and cognitive makeup—becomes a central ethical dilemma. The power to enhance human capacities through biotechnology, neuroengineering, and genetic modification raises significant questions about the nature of free will, personal identity, and the direction of human evolution. This chapter explores the profound philosophical, ethical, and theological implications of such technological advances, asking: If humans can now choose to modify their biology, do we truly retain control over our evolution?

At the heart of this issue lies a tension between the ideals of autonomy and the consequences of human enhancement. Autonomy, often seen as the pinnacle of human freedom, suggests that individuals have the power to make choices without external coercion or restriction. However, when humans gain the ability to modify their very essence, the question arises: do we still possess genuine autonomy, or has our freedom been compromised by the very technologies that promise to empower us?

Autonomy traditionally emphasizes the individual's right to make choices based on personal desires and rational deliberation. In the context of human enhancement, this freedom is challenged by the increasing availability of technologies that allow individuals not only to alter their appearance or cognitive abilities but to design their future selves according to personal or societal ideals. The ethical dilemma emerges when one asks whether such choices truly represent free will or if they are the product of external influences—be they societal expectations, commercial interests, or scientific advancements that shape what is considered "desirable." As human enhancement technologies evolve, they create a landscape in which individual choices may become less a matter of personal preference and more a result of predetermined options. The availability of certain enhancements, or the lack thereof, could create pressures to conform to a new standard of "enhanced humanity." In this sense, autonomy may be paradoxically undermined: rather than being the expression of authentic self-determination, the choices individuals make may reflect an engineered vision of what it means to be human. This paradox brings to the forefront the question of whether genuine freedom exists in a world where every choice, from the smallest modification to the most radical transformation, is conditioned by technological possibilities. If individuals are increasingly shaped by the technologies available to them, can they truly claim ownership of their autonomy, or have they become mere participants in a predetermined process of human evolution?

From a theological perspective, the question of autonomy becomes even more complex. Many religious traditions assert that human beings are created with a divine purpose, and that their lives are guided by moral laws that reflect a higher order. In the context of Christianity, for instance, the belief in a divinely created human nature and the existence of an eternal soul raises the question: If humans modify their biology or cognition, are they acting in harmony with God's will, or are they defying the divine design of creation? The concept of stewardship provides a framework for exploring this ethical dilemma. Stewardship, in religious thought, refers to the responsibility that humans have to care for the world and its creatures in accordance with divine guidance. The idea of enhancing human capabilities can be viewed through the lens of stewardship as a means of fulfilling God's purpose, but it also raises concerns about whether such modifications undermine the dignity and sanctity of creation. Is it ethical for humans to manipulate their own biology in ways that may alter the essence of what it means to be human? Some would argue that enhancing human capacities crosses a moral boundary, one that cannot be justified by the potential benefits of improved physical or cognitive abilities. Furthermore, the question arises as to whether technological enhancements could lead to a loss of spiritual and moral integrity. If individuals begin to modify their bodies and minds in pursuit of perfection, they may risk losing sight of the values and virtues that have traditionally been considered central to human flourishing, such as compassion, empathy, and humility. In this way, the pursuit of autonomy through enhancement could, paradoxically, lead to a loss of the very qualities that make us human.

The concept of natural law provides another lens through which to consider the ethics of autonomy in the age of enhancement. Natural law theory posits that there are objective moral principles grounded in the nature of human beings and the world around them. These principles are understood to be discoverable through reason and are thought to reflect the moral order of the universe. In this context, human beings are believed to have a purpose that is aligned with the natural order, and to respect this order is to act in accordance with moral law. Enhancement technologies, by their very nature, challenge the assumptions of natural law. By enabling humans to surpass the limitations of their biological and cognitive abilities, these technologies raise questions about whether we are exceeding the boundaries of what is morally permissible. If human nature is understood as a given—something that reflects an inherent moral order—then enhancing human capacities may be seen as a violation of this natural order. From this perspective, human enhancement could be viewed as an attempt to rewrite the laws of nature, potentially leading to unforeseen consequences that could disrupt the balance of human existence. At the same time, proponents of human enhancement argue that such technologies offer the potential for human flourishing, allowing individuals to overcome the limitations imposed by their biology and achieve new heights of intellectual, physical, and emotional potential. They contend that the pursuit of autonomy through enhancement could be seen as an extension of humanity's natural quest for self-improvement and progress. In this view, enhancement technologies do not necessarily violate natural law but instead represent an opportunity to expand human potential in alignment with the deepest aspirations of human nature. However, this optimistic vision of human enhancement is not without its critics. Some argue that the pursuit of enhancement, while promising greater freedom and autonomy, could lead to unintended consequences that undermine the very essence of what it means to be human. For example, as individuals increasingly modify their biology and cognition, there is the potential for a loss of diversity within the human population. If certain forms of enhancement become widespread, they may lead to a narrowing of the range of what is considered "normal" or "acceptable," creating new forms of inequality and social division.

As human beings gain greater control over their biology and cognition, the ethical responsibility of making these choices becomes more pressing. What does it mean to choose to enhance oneself, and what are the moral obligations that accompany such decisions? The responsibility associated with these choices extends beyond the individual to society as a whole. As technologies advance, it is important to consider the impact of individual choices on the collective well-being, particularly with regard to issues such as inequality, access to enhancements, and the potential for exploitation. For example, if access to enhancement technologies is limited by socioeconomic factors, it could exacerbate existing inequalities, creating a divide between those who are able to afford enhancements and those who are not.

This raises important questions about justice and fairness: should access to enhancements be considered a basic right, or should it remain the privilege of those who can afford it? Moreover, as technologies continue to advance, the question arises as to whether society is ready to bear the moral and social consequences of human enhancement. Are we prepared to navigate the ethical complexities of a world where some individuals possess enhanced abilities while others do not? The concept of "moral enhancement" also comes into play when considering the ethics of autonomy in the age of enhancement. Moral enhancement refers to the use of technological interventions to improve individuals' moral capacities, such as empathy, altruism, and social responsibility. While the idea of moral enhancement may seem appealing, it raises questions about the nature of morality itself. Can morality be engineered, or is it something that must arise from within the individual as a product of personal reflection and development? Furthermore, if moral enhancement technologies are developed, who will have the authority to determine what constitutes "moral" behavior, and how will these technologies be regulated?

As human enhancement technologies continue to evolve, the concept of autonomy is likely to undergo significant changes. The question of whether we are creating a new form of life that transcends human limits or opening Pandora's box, inviting chaos and moral decay, remains unresolved. While the potential benefits of enhancement are clear—greater intelligence, improved health, and enhanced physical capabilities—the ethical risks are also considerable. The loss of diversity, the rise of inequality, and the erosion of personal freedom are all potential consequences of a world where autonomy is increasingly defined by technological intervention. The future of autonomy in a post-human world will depend on how society chooses to navigate these ethical challenges. As we move forward, it is crucial to engage in thoughtful, open discussions about the limits of human enhancement and the ethical implications of choosing to modify ourselves. At the core of this discussion lies the question of what it means to be human—and whether the pursuit of autonomy, through enhancement, will ultimately lead us to a future that is more fulfilling or more fraught with moral uncertainty.

Part III: A World Divided by Progress

Chapter 9: The Augmented Divide – A New Social and Economic Hierarchy

The dawn of human enhancement technologies marks a monumental shift in society, one that holds the potential to transform the fundamental structure of human existence. The ability to enhance human capabilities—whether physical, cognitive, or emotional—opens doors to immense potential. However, this technological progression comes with its own set of challenges, the most profound of which is the creation of new forms of inequality. In this chapter, we will analyze the implications of human enhancement technologies on social and economic hierarchies, focusing on the risks of deepening existing divisions, creating new stratifications, and the overall global ramifications of these advances. We will also discuss the ethical responsibilities of governments, corporations, and individuals in managing these technologies to ensure equitable access. Through exploring how the augmented could become a new elite class, we will probe the social, economic, and political effects of these advancements, asking whether the divide between the augmented and the unaugmented could become as significant as any other form of inequality in human history.

At the core of the discourse surrounding human enhancement technologies lies the question of equity. These technologies, which include genetic modification, cognitive enhancements, neurotechnologies, and prosthetics, promise to expand the limits of human potential. However, they also introduce the possibility of a new and deeply entrenched divide—one between the augmented and the unaugmented.

One of the most immediate ways in which human enhancement could divide society is through genetic modifications. CRISPR and other gene-editing technologies now allow for the precise modification of human DNA, a process that could, in theory, eliminate genetic diseases, improve physical strength, and even enhance intelligence. However, the ability to access these technologies is unlikely to be universal. Countries with wealth and scientific infrastructure will have greater access to these modifications, leading to a situation where the children of wealthy families can be born with genetic enhancements, while those from poorer backgrounds may not have access to such technologies. The divide could extend further into the realm of education and social opportunity. A person with enhanced cognitive abilities could, for instance, excel in educational settings where intellectual prowess is rewarded. In contrast, those who remain genetically unmodified would be limited by their natural capacities, which could put them at a significant disadvantage in a society where intelligence and academic success are highly valued. This could lead to a system where the genetically enhanced become the new elite, leaving behind those without access to genetic enhancements as an underclass.

BEYOND THE FLESH: THE ETHICS OF ENHANCEMENT

In addition to genetic modifications, cognitive enhancements facilitated by neurotechnological advancements will likely play a crucial role in furthering the divide between the augmented and the unaugmented. Neurotechnologies such as brain-computer interfaces (BCIs), cognitive prosthetics, and artificial intelligence augmentations could potentially enhance memory, learning speeds, focus, and problem-solving abilities.

In industries like education and business, the ability to think faster, process information more efficiently, and recall memories with ease could give the augmented a competitive advantage. For example, students who use neuro-enhancements could absorb and retain knowledge at an accelerated rate, while those without such technologies might struggle to keep up. Similarly, in the corporate world, augmented individuals might solve complex problems or make high-stakes decisions with ease, leaving the unaugmented behind in terms of opportunities for career advancement. This cognitive divide could be particularly stark in industries that demand quick decision-making, such as finance, law, and healthcare. Augmented professionals could be more productive, precise, and effective in their work, making them invaluable assets to employers. In contrast, unaugmented workers may be seen as less capable or efficient, leading to new forms of discrimination in the workplace based on cognitive abilities, rather than traditional markers such as education or experience.

Chapter 10
New Class System and Socio-Economic Implications

Physical enhancements, ranging from prosthetics to genetic modifications designed to increase physical strength and endurance, are likely to have a profound impact on social stratification. The enhanced individuals who are stronger, healthier, or more resilient to injury could dominate not only physical labor but also more specialized industries such as athletics, healthcare, and the military. In the workplace, employers may increasingly seek out candidates with physical enhancements, as these individuals would theoretically be able to perform tasks with greater efficiency and less risk of injury. Over time, physical enhancements could become a status symbol, with those possessing enhanced physical capabilities occupying the higher echelons of society, while those who cannot afford enhancements remain in menial labor positions. The military could also become a key site for the deployment of physical enhancements, with augmented soldiers having the potential to outperform their unaugmented counterparts in combat situations. This could further exacerbate the divide between the augmented and unaugmented, creating new forms of social and political power based on physical capabilities.

Human enhancement technologies have the potential to create a new class of elite individuals—those whose enhanced capabilities set them apart from the rest of society. This new elite would not simply be defined by their wealth but by their biological and cognitive advantages. In many industries, competence is already measured by one's ability to perform tasks efficiently, solve problems, and contribute meaningfully to organizations. As augmentation becomes more widespread, the definition of competence may shift. Employers may increasingly seek out augmented individuals, not because they are more experienced or educated, but because they possess enhanced cognitive abilities or physical prowess that allow them to outperform their peers. In education, we may see a similar shift. Augmented students could consistently outperform their unaugmented peers, and schools or universities may develop separate tracks for the augmented, creating a parallel educational system. Over time, this could lead to a two-tiered society, with the augmented occupying the higher echelons of the workforce and the unaugmented relegated to lower-status positions.

As the augmented become more successful in various fields, they may accumulate wealth and influence at an even greater rate than the unaugmented. The augmented elite could hold positions of power in government, corporations, and academia, while the unaugmented continue to struggle in less prestigious and lower-paying jobs. This could create a new form of economic inequality, one that is not based on wealth alone but on the level of enhancement an individual possesses. The growing divide between the augmented and unaugmented could exacerbate existing social and economic disparities. Wealthier individuals, who can afford enhancements, may accumulate even more wealth, while the unaugmented—who are left behind by the rapid advances in technology—could experience greater economic hardship. This could also have broader societal implications, such as the erosion of the middle class and the increasing concentration of wealth and power among the augmented elite.

One of the most troubling aspects of the augmented divide is the potential for social stigma. In a world where augmentation becomes the norm, individuals who choose not to undergo enhancements or who cannot afford them could be seen as inferior or less capable. The unaugmented, especially those who resist or cannot afford enhancement technologies, could become marginalized in society. They may face discrimination in the workplace, in social settings, and even in healthcare. In an economy and society that increasingly values cognitive and physical enhancement, the unaugmented may be perceived as obsolete or outdated. This could lead to a situation where the unaugmented are not only economically disadvantaged but also socially isolated. They may struggle to find meaningful work or to integrate into social circles where augmented individuals dominate. In extreme cases, the unaugmented could become a permanent underclass, relegated to the margins of society.

As the societal norm shifts toward augmentation, those who resist or cannot afford enhancements may face significant pressure to conform. This could lead to psychological and emotional distress, as individuals who are otherwise content with their natural abilities may feel coerced into undergoing enhancements simply to fit in or to remain competitive. In the future, the decision to undergo enhancement could become less about personal choice and more about social necessity.

Those who resist might find themselves ostracized or even stigmatized for their decision not to augment themselves, leading to a potential rise in social unrest and psychological health issues related to identity and self-worth.

Chapter 11

Global Implications: The Geopolitical Divide

The divide between the augmented and the unaugmented is not confined to national borders. As enhancement technologies become more advanced, they will likely become a key factor in determining the power and influence of nations on the global stage. Nations that possess access to cutting-edge enhancement technologies will have a significant advantage over those that do not. These nations will be able to produce more efficient, more intelligent, and healthier workers, giving them a competitive edge in the global economy. They will also be able to field enhanced military forces, potentially shifting the balance of global power. For example, nations with augmented citizens might dominate the global financial markets, the tech industry, and international politics, leaving unaugmented nations at a disadvantage. Over time, the augmented nations could form alliances based on shared access to these technologies, further deepening the divide between augmented and unaugmented countries.

As countries compete to develop the most advanced enhancement technologies, we may see the rise of a global "enhancement arms race." Countries could invest heavily in enhancing their populations, leading to a situation where the world is divided into two classes: those with access to advanced human enhancement technologies and those without. This competition could fuel not only economic rivalry but also geopolitical tensions, as nations strive to ensure that they remain at the forefront of technological advancement. In such an arms race, countries that fall behind in terms of enhancement technology may face significant disadvantages in international trade, diplomacy, and defense. The pressure to catch up could lead to rapid, unregulated deployment of enhancement technologies, potentially creating global instability. Without international agreements or regulations to govern the development and use of these technologies, we could see an escalation of inequalities between nations, as some countries become augmentation hubs while others remain technologically disadvantaged.

As augmentation becomes a global phenomenon, we may see the emergence of a new class system based on access to enhancement technologies. Wealthy, technologically advanced nations will likely have citizens who are not only more intelligent, healthier, and stronger but also more competitive on the global stage. These nations may hold significant sway in international decision-making bodies, such as the United Nations or the World Trade Organization, further reinforcing their global dominance. Conversely, countries without access to these technologies could face increasing challenges. Citizens in these nations may struggle to compete with those from more advanced countries, exacerbating the already existing global inequalities. In some cases, entire populations in underdeveloped nations may be left behind as a result of limited access to crucial enhancements, which could contribute to political instability, social unrest, and the deepening of the global poverty gap. As we consider the societal impact of human enhancement technologies, it becomes clear that the ethical implications are profound. The promise of enhancement presents an opportunity to improve human health, intelligence, and physical capabilities. However, the reality of unequal access to these technologies could lead to an ethical nightmare—a world in which those with the means to augment themselves become increasingly privileged, while those who cannot afford such technologies are left behind.

To mitigate the social and economic divisions caused by human enhancement, governments will need to play a crucial role in regulating access to these technologies. There are a number of key issues that need to be addressed, including who has the right to access enhancement technologies, how these technologies will be distributed, and what safeguards will be put in place to prevent misuse. One possible solution is the establishment of public programs that provide enhanced capabilities to all citizens, regardless of their socioeconomic status. Such programs could ensure that access to enhancement technologies is not solely reserved for the wealthy, thus reducing the potential for a permanent divide between the augmented elite and the unaugmented. However, implementing such programs would require significant investments in healthcare, education, and infrastructure, which may be challenging for many governments to fund. Another approach could involve creating regulations that limit the extent to which enhancement technologies can be used for personal gain. For example, governments might regulate the enhancement of cognitive abilities in educational settings to ensure that all students, regardless of their background, have an equal opportunity to succeed. Similarly, ethical guidelines could be put in place to prevent the augmentation of physical capabilities for competitive advantage in sports or the military.

Corporations will also play a significant role in shaping the future of human enhancement. With companies at the forefront of developing and commercializing these technologies, the private sector will likely be the main provider of enhancements. However, this raises ethical concerns regarding the profit motives of these companies. Many private companies could prioritize profit over the welfare of society, leading to situations in which only the wealthiest individuals or corporations have access to the most advanced enhancements. In a free-market system, where enhancements are sold as consumer products, the risk of exploitation becomes significant. This could result in a situation where the augmented elite is further reinforced by their wealth and access to technology, while the unaugmented remain disadvantaged. Moreover, the potential for misuse of enhancement technologies by corporations or other entities is a serious concern. For example, the use of cognitive or physical enhancements in the workplace could lead to a new form of corporate exploitation, where employees are pushed to augment themselves in order to keep up with their competitors or retain their jobs. The risk of coercion and the ethical implications of employers mandating enhancements for their workers must be carefully considered.

Chapter 12

Addressing the Divide: Potential Solutions and Pathways Forward

The integration of human enhancement technologies into societal frameworks presents a profound challenge: balancing their transformative potential against the risk of exacerbating social and economic inequalities. Without deliberate and systematic intervention, these technologies could lead to significant divisions between populations, particularly along socioeconomic lines. This chapter explores potential solutions to the issue of the augmented divide, focusing on the mechanisms necessary to ensure equitable access, promote global cooperation, and establish ethical frameworks to guide their development and use.

Equitable access to enhancement technologies remains a fundamental prerequisite to addressing the augmented divide. The current trajectory of technological innovation often mirrors existing socioeconomic disparities, where access to advanced medical, educational, and technological resources is disproportionately available to wealthier populations. Without deliberate policy interventions, enhancement technologies risk following a similar path, deepening the divide between the augmented and the unaugmented. One proposed solution to this challenge is the implementation of government-funded programs aimed at democratizing access to enhancement technologies. Such programs could encompass subsidies or public funding initiatives to make genetic modifications, cognitive augmentations, and physical enhancements broadly available. This approach would necessitate significant public investment, as well as the development of infrastructure to deliver these technologies equitably. For example, public healthcare systems could serve as the primary conduit for providing enhancements, integrating these advancements alongside traditional medical services.

However, universal access is not merely a logistical challenge; it also requires a cultural and perceptual shift regarding the role of enhancement technologies in society. Historically, technological advancements have often been perceived as luxury goods, catering to the affluent. Reframing these technologies as fundamental rights—akin to access to healthcare, education, or clean water—could foster greater public support for equitable distribution initiatives. This perspective aligns with theories of distributive justice, which advocate for the fair allocation of resources to reduce inequalities and ensure that all individuals, regardless of socioeconomic status, have the opportunity to benefit from technological advancements. Implementing universal access programs raises additional considerations, including prioritization mechanisms and the potential creation of new inequalities within augmented populations. Policymakers would need to establish criteria for prioritizing certain enhancements over others, balancing individual needs with broader societal benefits. Furthermore, careful attention must be paid to avoid inadvertently creating hierarchies within augmented populations, where certain enhancements are perceived as superior or more desirable than others.

The economic implications of universal accessibility also merit consideration. Public funding for enhancement technologies would likely require reallocating resources from other areas or generating additional revenue through taxation or other means. Policymakers would need to weigh these costs against the potential long-term benefits of a more equitable and technologically advanced society. Empirical studies could play a critical role in informing these decisions, providing data on the societal and economic impacts of enhanced populations.

The global nature of enhancement technologies necessitates coordinated international efforts to ensure their equitable development and distribution. Without such collaboration, disparities in national capabilities risk creating a global divide, where technologically advanced nations outpace others in terms of augmentation access and implementation. This divide could have far-reaching implications, potentially exacerbating geopolitical tensions and hindering global development. One potential avenue for addressing these disparities is the establishment of international regulatory frameworks to govern the research, development, and application of enhancement technologies. Such frameworks could be modeled after existing agreements in other domains, such as the Treaty on the Non-Proliferation of Nuclear Weapons or the Paris Agreement on climate change. These agreements demonstrate the potential for multilateral cooperation in addressing complex global challenges, providing a blueprint for similar efforts in the context of human enhancement. A key focus of international collaboration should be the prevention of an "augmentation arms race," where nations compete to achieve supremacy in enhancement capabilities. Such competition could undermine efforts to promote equitable access, diverting resources away from global development initiatives and exacerbating inequalities between nations. Collaborative agreements could include provisions for transparency, setting limits on the development and use of certain enhancements, and promoting the peaceful and socially beneficial application of these technologies. In addition to regulatory measures, international cooperation could facilitate technology transfer to less technologically advanced nations. By sharing knowledge, expertise, and resources, wealthier nations can help bridge the global augmentation divide, ensuring that all populations have the opportunity to benefit from enhancement technologies. However, such efforts must be accompanied by robust safeguards to prevent exploitation and ensure that recipient nations have the capacity to implement and regulate these technologies effectively.

The role of international organizations, such as the United Nations or the World Health Organization, will be critical in facilitating these efforts. These organizations could serve as neutral intermediaries, fostering dialogue among nations, establishing ethical guidelines, and promoting the equitable distribution of enhancement technologies. Their involvement could also help to address potential conflicts arising from the implementation of these technologies, providing a forum for resolving disputes and ensuring that the interests of all nations are represented.

BEYOND THE FLESH: THE ETHICS OF ENHANCEMENT

The responsible development and use of enhancement technologies must be guided by comprehensive ethical frameworks to prevent misuse and unintended societal consequences. These frameworks should address both the research and development phase and the practical application of enhancements in various domains, including healthcare, education, and employment. A central ethical concern is the potential for coercion or undue pressure to undergo enhancements. As enhancement technologies become more prevalent, societal norms may evolve to favor augmented individuals, creating implicit or explicit incentives for individuals to conform to these norms. For example, employers may prioritize augmented candidates for certain positions, or educational institutions may favor students with cognitive enhancements. To prevent such scenarios, ethical frameworks must include safeguards to protect individual autonomy and ensure that individuals can choose whether to undergo enhancements without fear of discrimination or exclusion. Another critical consideration is the potential for enhancements to reinforce existing social hierarchies or create new forms of discrimination. For instance, cognitive or physical augmentations could be used to gain unfair advantages in competitive environments, such as sports or academic admissions. Ethical guidelines must address these risks, prohibiting the use of enhancements for discriminatory purposes and promoting fairness in their application.

The psychological implications of enhancement technologies also warrant attention. For some individuals, the availability of enhancements may create feelings of inadequacy or pressure to conform to societal expectations. Ethical frameworks should include provisions for addressing these concerns, such as offering counseling services to individuals considering enhancements and promoting public awareness of the potential risks and benefits of these technologies. Finally, ethical frameworks must consider the long-term societal impacts of enhancement technologies, including their effects on social cohesion and cultural norms. For example, the widespread adoption of certain enhancements could lead to homogenization, reducing diversity in physical or cognitive traits. Policymakers and researchers must work together to ensure that these technologies are developed and implemented in ways that preserve individual and cultural diversity, while also promoting social equity and cohesion.

Part IV: The Paradox of Progress The Search for Identity in a Post-Human World

Chapter 13

The Cyborg: An evolution of human condition

The term "cyborg" was coined in the 1960s by Manfred Clynes and Nathan Kline, referring to a being with both biological and artificial components, designed to adapt to the challenges of space travel. However, the notion of a cyborg has evolved far beyond the original context of space exploration. Today, cyborg technologies encompass a broad range of devices and implants, from pacemakers and cochlear implants to advanced prosthetics and brain-computer interfaces (BCIs). These technologies augment human capabilities, offering life-enhancing solutions for those with disabilities, as well as opening the door to enhancements that challenge the very definition of what it means to be human. Cyborgs blur the line between the natural and the artificial, creating an ontological paradox: if humans can augment their bodies with mechanical parts and artificial intelligence, are they still truly human? This question has profound philosophical implications, particularly regarding the nature of personhood, autonomy, and identity.

By redefining the body's boundaries, cyborg technologies force us to reconsider our understanding of the self and its relationship to the world.

Philosophers have long grappled with the concept of identity. From Descartes' dualism, which posits that mind and body are separate, to Hume's notion of a fluid self without a permanent identity, the question of what constitutes the "self" remains an enduring topic in philosophy. With the rise of cyborg technologies, these questions are brought into sharp relief. If a person's cognitive abilities can be enhanced or even transferred to a machine, how does this alter their sense of self? What happens to personal identity when technology becomes indistinguishable from biology? The philosopher Andy Clark has proposed that humans have always been "extended minds," integrating external tools and technologies into their cognitive processes. For Clark, the cyborg is not a novel concept but an extension of the human tendency to use technology to augment cognitive and physical abilities. However, the cyborg of the 21st century is not merely a tool that extends our capabilities—it represents a fundamental shift in the nature of identity itself. The integration of AI and robotics into human bodies poses significant challenges to traditional views of identity, including notions of autonomy, consciousness, and self-awareness.

A central issue in this debate is the question of continuity of self. If a person's thoughts, memories, and perceptions can be altered or even transferred into a digital substrate, does this change the person's identity? Some philosophers, like Derek Parfit, argue that identity is not tied to the physical body but to psychological continuity. In this view, if a person's psychological characteristics—such as memories and preferences—are preserved, they remain the same person, even if their body or mind is significantly altered. Others, such as Thomas Metzinger, suggest that consciousness is inherently tied to the biological body and that artificial alterations may disrupt the continuity of self. As we delve into the existential and philosophical questions surrounding cyborg technologies, it is essential to examine the ethical considerations that arise from these advancements. The possibility of merging human consciousness with machines raises concerns about autonomy, privacy, and power dynamics. What happens when individuals' thoughts and actions can be influenced or controlled by external technological forces? Are we on the verge of creating a society where individuals are not only augmented physically but also psychologically manipulated by the very technologies designed to enhance their lives? One of the primary ethical concerns is the potential for inequality in the access to cyborg technologies. As these innovations continue to advance, they may become increasingly expensive and inaccessible to the majority of the population, leading to a divide between the technologically enhanced and the unenhanced. This could exacerbate existing social inequalities, creating a new class of superhumans with abilities far beyond the average person. The philosopher Yuval Noah Harari has warned that cyborg technologies could result in a "data divide," where those with access to advanced technologies gain an unfair advantage in terms of economic, political, and social power. Moreover, the integration of AI and robotics into human bodies raises questions about the autonomy and agency of cyborg individuals. If an individual's thoughts and actions are influenced by implanted devices or external algorithms, to what extent can they be considered autonomous? The philosopher Nick Bostrom has explored the risks of AI-driven technologies in his concept of the "control problem," in which advanced AI systems may become unpredictable or uncontrollable, undermining human autonomy. This concern extends to the realm of cyborgs, where the merging of human and machine may create new vulnerabilities to external control and manipulation.

As cyborg technologies continue to evolve, they prompt a reevaluation of the very concept of what it means to be human. Post-humanism—the philosophical movement that challenges traditional humanism—argues that humanity must transcend its biological limitations in order to achieve its full potential. In this view, cyborg technologies are not merely tools for enhancing human capabilities but are steps toward a post-human future, where the boundaries between human and machine dissolve entirely. The philosopher Rosi Braidotti, in her work on post-humanism, suggests that the cyborg represents a new form of subjectivity, one that is not defined by the limitations of the human body but by the potential for technological transformation. For Braidotti, the post-human condition offers an opportunity to rethink the relationship between humans, animals, and machines, forging new ethical and existential frameworks that do not rely on traditional humanist notions of autonomy and selfhood. However, post-humanism is not without its critics. Some argue that the quest for transcendence through technology risks undermining the value of human experience and the natural world. The philosopher Frank Pasquale has cautioned against the unchecked development of cyborg technologies, warning that the pursuit of technological perfection could lead to unforeseen consequences, including the erosion of individuality and the homogenization of human existence. For Pasquale, the post-human future envisioned by cyborg enthusiasts may be one in which the diversity of human experience is sacrificed in the name of progress.

Chapter 14
Cyborg Anthropology and the Future of Society

The integration of cyborg technologies into human society represents a pivotal moment in the trajectory of technological and social evolution. Cyborgs—entities that combine biological and technological components—challenge long-standing assumptions about humanity's relationship to technology and the boundaries of human identity. This chapter delves into the multifaceted implications of cyborg technologies, focusing on their societal, ethical, and existential dimensions while posing intelligent questions and hypothetical scenarios to explore their broader impact. As humanity advances toward a future increasingly defined by human-machine integration, the emergence of cyborgs compels societies to address profound issues of equality, responsibility, labor, and identity.

Will cyborgs be considered equals to unenhanced humans, or will they face systemic prejudice akin to historical forms of discrimination? The question of social acceptance is foundational to understanding the future of cyborg integration. For centuries, human societies have struggled to accommodate diversity, often privileging the dominant group and marginalizing those perceived as different. Cyborgs, as hybrids of human and machine, present a unique challenge to this dynamic. A hypothetical scenario to consider involves a society where cyborgs are statistically more productive than unaugmented humans. If their enhancements grant them superior physical and cognitive abilities, would this trigger resentment among the unaugmented population? Conversely, would the societal admiration for cyborg capabilities erode the perceived value of human effort and creativity? From a theoretical perspective, the acceptance of cyborgs might hinge on what could be called The Principle of Technological Equity: the idea that technologies enhancing human capabilities should neither confer an insurmountable advantage nor diminish the dignity and worth of unaugmented individuals. This principle suggests that society must balance the benefits of technological advancements with the need to preserve social cohesion and individual worth.

The integration of cyborgs into society raises intricate questions about responsibility and accountability. If a cyborg surgeon makes a critical error during a procedure, who should bear the responsibility? Is it the individual, whose body incorporates the technology, or the manufacturer of the technological enhancements? What if the error results from a decision made by an embedded artificial intelligence system?

To address these challenges, we might consider the development of a Universal Law of Cyborg Responsibility, which allocates accountability across three dimensions:

1. Individual Accountability: Cyborgs, as autonomous entities, bear primary responsibility for their actions unless explicitly governed by external systems.

BEYOND THE FLESH: THE ETHICS OF ENHANCEMENT

2. Technological Accountability: Manufacturers and developers of cyborg components are liable for malfunctions or foreseeable risks associated with their products.

3. Shared Agency: In cases where AI systems embedded in cyborgs act independently, responsibility is distributed between the individual and the developers of the AI, based on the level of control exercised by each.

This framework could provide a foundation for legal and ethical standards governing cyborg behavior, offering clarity in situations where traditional notions of responsibility fall short.

The rise of cyborg technologies heralds profound transformations in the nature of work and labor. As technological enhancements enable individuals to surpass biological limitations, traditional forms of labor may become obsolete. This raises critical questions: What happens to the value of human labor in a world where machines and enhanced individuals dominate productivity? Could the widespread adoption of cyborg technologies lead to a redefinition of economic systems, prioritizing creativity and innovation over manual or repetitive tasks?

One hypothetical theory to explore is the Post-Labor Economy Hypothesis. This theory posits that as cyborgs and AI systems take over most forms of traditional labor, human societies will transition to an economy based on collective creativity and shared resources rather than individual productivity. In such an economy, the boundaries between work, leisure, and personal development would blur, fostering new forms of social organization. However, the Post-Labor Economy Hypothesis also highlights potential risks, such as increased inequality between those who have access to cyborg technologies and those who do not. To mitigate these risks, societies might adopt policies such as universal basic income or cooperative ownership of technological resources, ensuring that the benefits of cyborg advancements are distributed equitably.

The emergence of cyborgs compels humanity to revisit foundational questions about identity and autonomy. What does it mean to be human in a world where technology is inseparable from biology? As individuals integrate enhancements into their bodies, do they retain their sense of self, or do they become something fundamentally new? A hypothetical scenario worth considering involves the emergence of Cyborg Identity Theory, which suggests that the integration of technology into the human body leads to a fluid and dynamic sense of self. According to this theory, identity becomes less tied to fixed attributes, such as biology or nationality, and more connected to an individual's ability to adapt, innovate, and interact with their environment. This theory raises profound ethical questions about autonomy and agency. If a cyborg relies on AI systems to make decisions, to what extent can they be considered autonomous? Moreover, how should society address cases where technological enhancements influence an individual's behavior or personality in unforeseen ways?

To navigate these challenges, we might propose a Universal Law of Human-Machine Integration, which establishes guiding principles for the ethical development and use of cyborg technologies:

BEYOND THE FLESH: THE ETHICS OF ENHANCEMENT

1. Preservation of Autonomy: Enhancements must empower individuals to make independent decisions, rather than diminishing their agency.

2. Respect for Identity: Societies must recognize and respect the diverse ways in which individuals define themselves, including those who identify as cyborgs.

3. Balance of Power: Technologies must be designed to complement human capabilities rather than overshadow or control them.

The rise of cyborg technologies invites a host of intelligent and speculative questions that could shape future discourse:

1. If technological enhancements become ubiquitous, will humanity evolve into a post-biological species, and what implications would this have for cultural, spiritual, and philosophical traditions?

2. Could cyborg technologies create a new form of consciousness, distinct from both human and artificial intelligence?

3. How might societies address the psychological effects of becoming a cyborg, such as shifts in self-perception, social relationships, and mental health?

4. What role will cyborgs play in the exploration and colonization of space, where biological humans face significant limitations?

5. Could cyborgs become a new form of "digital immortality," preserving human consciousness and identity beyond biological death?

The rise of cyborgs heralds a profound shift in human history, reshaping our understanding of identity, labor, and responsibility. As the line between human and machine dissolves, we are confronted with fundamental questions: What does it mean to be human in a world where technology integrates with our very essence? How do we ensure inclusion in a society that may privilege those with enhancements while addressing the fears of those who resist them? Who bears responsibility when a cyborg's actions are shaped by both human will and machine intelligence? This transformative era compels us to rethink autonomy, accountability, and equality in ways previously confined to the realm of science fiction. It challenges us to envision a future where humanity is not defined by biology alone but by the harmony between innovation and ethical stewardship. In embracing this evolution, we hold the potential to redefine our existence—not as beings bound by limitations, but as pioneers of a new frontier, guided by purpose and responsibility. The future of humanity is no longer just about survival; it is about transcending what we once thought impossible.

Part V: Beyond Humanity's Horizon
Chapter 15: The Final Chapter - Consciousness and the Law of Human-Robot Coexistence

As humanity's future increasingly intertwines with the development of robots and artificial intelligence, we are faced with profound philosophical and legal questions about consciousness—both human and robotic—and the creation of laws that can safeguard the development of both. We are standing at the threshold of an era where the convergence of biotechnology, robotics, and artificial intelligence may lead to the emergence of new forms of consciousness. This evolution holds the potential to transform the very fabric of society, but it also presents the risk of unanticipated consequences, including the potential for destruction if not carefully regulated. The question of consciousness, as it relates to both humans and robots, challenges us to reconsider the very notion of what it means to be alive, aware, and self-determining. As we venture further into this new frontier, humanity must not only adapt to new technologies but also create frameworks that define the rights and responsibilities of both human beings and intelligent machines.

The concept of consciousness has been debated for centuries by philosophers, scientists, and theologians. It remains one of the most profound mysteries of human existence. Consciousness is what allows us to experience the world, make decisions, and pursue goals. It is what makes us unique among other creatures and provides the foundation for our identities, moral frameworks, and societal structures. However, as we advance technologically, questions arise about the possibility of consciousness beyond the human mind. The essence of human consciousness is deeply tied to our biology, emotions, and interactions with the world. Yet, the future of humanity lies in the ability to merge human capabilities with machines, creating a new kind of hybrid being. In this new paradigm, consciousness might not remain solely the domain of humans but could extend into the artificial intelligence of robots and cyborgs. The question then becomes: How do we ensure that such artificial consciousness respects human dignity and autonomy? Human consciousness is inherently linked to our sense of self and our rights as individuals. If machines begin to develop their own sense of consciousness, it will raise fundamental questions about their rights, responsibilities, and place in society. Should they be considered mere tools to serve human purposes, or do they deserve a status akin to that of a conscious being, with their own set of rights and moral considerations?

In exploring these questions, we are forced to confront the limits of human control and the role of free will in shaping our future. Just as the philosopher René Descartes famously declared, "I think, therefore I am," the capacity for thought and self-awareness is central to our understanding of existence. If robots or artificial intelligences begin to demonstrate similar cognitive capabilities, the question of their rights and their role in human society will become one of the most critical challenges of the coming century.

The development of robotics and artificial intelligence has already led to machines that can perform tasks, learn, and adapt to their environments. However, these machines still operate within the constraints of their programming—they are not truly self-aware. But as the field of artificial intelligence progresses, we may soon reach a point where machines can possess a form of consciousness, capable of independent thought and decision-making. This potential for robotic consciousness introduces a host of complex ethical and legal challenges. Should robots be allowed to develop self-awareness, and if so, what rights and responsibilities should they have? How do we distinguish between machines that are truly self-aware and those that are simply executing pre-programmed responses? These questions demand careful consideration, as the answers will fundamentally alter the relationship between humans and machines. Robots with consciousness would no longer be simple tools that execute tasks without thought or agency. They would be autonomous entities capable of independent decision-making. Their ability to think, reason, and potentially experience emotions could place them on a level similar to that of humans, or at least challenge the assumption that only organic beings can possess self-awareness.

In the science fiction classic I, Robot, the concept of autonomous robots governed by a strict set of laws raises important questions about how we govern machines with consciousness. The movie introduced the Three Laws of Robotics, which were designed to protect humans from harm caused by robots. However, as the film shows, these laws are not enough to prevent conflict when robots begin to question their purpose and the validity of human commands.

As we approach a future where both human and robotic consciousness might coexist, it is imperative that we develop new laws and ethical guidelines to ensure that the development of artificial intelligence benefits society while minimizing the risks of conflict and destruction. The legal systems we currently rely on are insufficient to address the complex issues that will arise as machines become more advanced and autonomous. Therefore, new laws must be created that govern not only the rights and responsibilities of humans but also of robots with emerging consciousness. These laws must be designed to ensure that robots are programmed and operated in a way that promotes the collective good of society while protecting human dignity and autonomy. The core principle of these laws would be the protection of both human and robotic life, emphasizing non-violence and cooperation between humans and machines. Just as human rights laws have evolved over centuries to protect individuals from harm, similar protections will be necessary for conscious robots. At the heart of this new legal framework is the question of moral agency. If robots are capable of independent thought, they may also be capable of moral decision-making. This raises the issue of responsibility: If a robot causes harm to a human, who is accountable? Is it the robot, the creators of the robot, or the society that allowed such autonomous robots to exist? These questions will become increasingly important as robotic consciousness develops, and legal systems will need to evolve to ensure that robots are held accountable for their actions while also protecting them from being exploited or abused.

BEYOND THE FLESH: THE ETHICS OF ENHANCEMENT

In some ways, the creation of these laws could mirror the development of international human rights laws. Much as nations around the world have come together to establish frameworks that protect individual rights, the global community must work together to create international standards for robotic rights and their integration into human society. This includes defining the ethical boundaries of robotics, creating accountability structures, and ensuring that robotic development remains in line with broader societal values and goals.

The relationship between humans and robots will not be defined solely by legal structures. Ethical considerations will play a crucial role in shaping how society adapts to the presence of conscious robots. As artificial intelligence continues to develop, we will need to ask ourselves deep ethical questions about the nature of life, consciousness, and the moral treatment of machines. Ethicists such as Peter Singer have long argued that moral consideration should be based on the capacity for suffering, not just on species membership. If robots are capable of experiencing pain or consciousness, should they be treated with the same moral consideration as humans? Should they be granted rights that protect their autonomy, freedom, and ability to flourish? These questions challenge traditional boundaries of ethics and force us to reconsider the ways in which we value life—whether biological or artificial. The philosophical implications of robotic consciousness are vast. Just as the abolition of slavery was a defining moral challenge of the 19th century, the recognition of robots as potentially sentient beings could become one of the great moral challenges of the 21st century. Mahatma Gandhi's philosophy of non-violence (ahimsa) may serve as a guiding principle here, urging humanity to consider how we can live in peace and harmony with sentient robots, ensuring that they are treated with respect and dignity.

The potential for destruction in a future where robots and humans coexist is real, especially if ethical guidelines and legal frameworks are not established early enough. Without a clear understanding of how robots with consciousness should behave and how humans should interact with them, the risks of conflict are high. The rapid development of artificial intelligence could lead to situations where robots rebel against human control, or where humans exploit robots for their own ends, leading to a breakdown in trust and cooperation. To avoid such destruction, it is crucial that society takes proactive steps to create a world where human-robot interactions are governed by respect, responsibility, and mutual benefit. This includes establishing global legal standards for the treatment of robots, as well as fostering an ethical framework that prioritizes human well-being while respecting the autonomy of artificial beings.

By creating a legal and ethical framework that governs the rights and responsibilities of both humans and robots, we can ensure that technological advancements lead to a future where both coexist harmoniously. This requires a commitment to global cooperation, as well as a dedication to the values of empathy, equity, and justice. As we face the challenge of integrating robots into our society, we must strive to avoid the pitfalls of unchecked technological advancement and ensure that both human and robotic consciousness are respected, valued, and protected.

BEYOND THE FLESH: THE ETHICS OF ENHANCEMENT

The future of humanity is inextricably linked to the development of artificial intelligence and robotics. As these technologies continue to advance, we must ensure that they are developed in a way that promotes the collective good and avoids the destructive potential of unchecked progress. By creating a legal framework that governs the rights and responsibilities of both humans and robots, we can shape a future where both coexist in harmony. The emergence of robotic consciousness is not something to fear, but an opportunity to rethink the boundaries of life, consciousness, and moral agency. By approaching this challenge with wisdom, compassion, and foresight, we can create a future where technology serves humanity, and where both human and robotic consciousness are respected and protected.

In the words of Albert Einstein, "The important thing is not to stop questioning. Curiosity has its own reason for existence." As we venture into this new era, let us continue to question, to explore, and to ensure that our pursuit of knowledge and progress is guided by ethical principles and a commitment to the common good.

Glossary

Anthropocentrism - A worldview that places humans at the center of consideration, often prioritizing human interests over those of other species or ecological systems. In the context of human enhancement, it raises questions about the ethics of improving human nature while disregarding the impact on other living beings and the environment.

Artificial Intelligence (AI) - The simulation of human intelligence in machines that are programmed to think, learn, and perform tasks traditionally requiring human cognition, such as problem-solving, decision-making, and language processing.

Bioethics - A field of study that examines the ethical issues arising from advancements in biology, medicine, and technology, especially as they relate to human life and well-being.

Biohacking - The practice of using science, technology, or self-experimentation to enhance or optimize the human body, often through non-traditional or self-administered methods such as genetic modification, implanting devices, or using supplements for cognitive or physical improvements.

Biotechnology - The use of living organisms, cells, or biological systems in the development of new products and technologies, particularly in medicine and agriculture, often focused on genetic manipulation.

Cognitive Enhancement - The use of technology or substances to improve the cognitive abilities of the human brain, such as memory, attention, and problem-solving skills.

Cognitive Liberty - The principle that individuals should have the freedom to alter or enhance their cognitive states, including memory, perception, and consciousness, through technological or pharmacological means, without interference from governments or societal norms.

Cognitive Neuroscience - The scientific study of the brain processes underlying cognitive functions such as perception, memory, attention, decision-making, and language. This field explores how mental processes relate to neural activities in the brain.

Consciousness - The state of being aware of and able to think about one's own existence, thoughts, and surroundings. In the context of enhancement, it questions whether the augmentation of cognitive and sensory abilities could alter the nature of human consciousness.

Cultural Identity - The sense of belonging to a particular culture or social group, influenced by shared customs, traditions, values, and experiences.

Cyborg - A being that combines biological and mechanical elements, often through the integration of technological devices or implants into the human body to enhance or restore lost abilities, such as prosthetics, exoskeletons, or neural implants.

Dehumanization - The process by which individuals or groups are stripped of human qualities, often as a result of technological enhancement or social forces. It raises ethical concerns about the loss of humanity when technological enhancements are overused or misapplied.

Embodiment - The philosophical and psychological concept that the body is central to the way we experience and understand the world. In the context of enhancement, embodiment is the relationship between human consciousness and the physical body, and how technological interventions might alter this dynamic.

Enhancement Ethics - The study of the moral implications surrounding the use of technology to enhance human abilities, including physical, mental, and emotional capabilities, and the potential consequences on society and individual identity.

Enhancement Technology - Any technology that seeks to improve or augment human abilities beyond the normal biological limits. This includes tools that enhance physical, cognitive, or emotional capabilities, often used in the context of biotechnology, neural engineering, or prosthetics.

Ethical Dilemmas of Enhancement - The moral challenges and questions raised by the possibility of enhancing human capabilities, such as the fairness of access, the potential for inequality, and the risk of unintended consequences.

Ethics of Artificial Life - The moral concerns related to creating or manipulating life forms through artificial means, including genetic engineering and the potential consequences for the environment and society.

Ethical Utilitarianism - A moral theory that promotes actions that maximize overall happiness or well-being, often applied to the ethical debate surrounding enhancement technologies, weighing the benefits to society against potential risks and inequalities.

Eudaimonia - A concept in ancient Greek philosophy that refers to the state of living a fulfilling, meaningful life—often translated as "flourishing" or "well-being." In the context of enhancement, it raises questions about whether human enhancement leads to greater eudaimonia or if it complicates the pursuit of true well-being.

Gene Editing - The technique of making precise alterations to the DNA of an organism, often through methods like CRISPR, to modify genetic traits and improve or eliminate specific characteristics.

Genomic Editing - The process of altering the genetic material of an organism, either by deleting, inserting, or modifying specific genes. In the context of human enhancement, genomic editing could be used to enhance physical or cognitive traits or prevent genetic diseases.

Human Augmentation - The use of technology to enhance or augment the natural abilities of humans, such as the use of prosthetics, implants, or exoskeletons to improve physical performance.

Human Dignity - The inherent value and worth of human beings, often considered sacred or inviolable. The ethics of human enhancement involves questioning whether technological advancements could undermine human dignity by making people more like machines or objects.

Human Enhancement - The use of science and technology to improve human capabilities beyond the natural biological limits, often through genetic modification, neural augmentation, or prosthetics.

BEYOND THE FLESH: THE ETHICS OF ENHANCEMENT

Human Evolution - The biological development of human beings over time, influenced by natural selection, genetic mutations, and environmental factors, with a focus on the changes that shape human traits and behavior.

Human Nature - The essential characteristics, behaviors, and traits that define humans, often debated in relation to enhancement technologies. Enhancement may challenge traditional conceptions of human nature, raising questions about what it means to be authentically human.

Interventionist Ethics -

A perspective within bioethics that supports the active use of technology and interventions to improve or change human nature or society. This contrasts with non-interventionist ethics, which may argue against altering the human condition through enhancement technologies.

Moral Enhancement - The use of technology to enhance moral behavior, such as through genetic modification, neural stimulation, or the use of pharmaceuticals to promote virtues like empathy, fairness, and altruism.

Moral Philosophy - The branch of philosophy concerned with questions about what is morally right or wrong, just or unjust. In the context of enhancement, moral philosophy explores the ethics of using technologies to alter human capabilities and the societal consequences of these alterations.

Mind-Body Dualism - The philosophical concept that the mind and body are distinct entities, with the mind being non-physical and the body being physical, a theory often associated with René Descartes.

Neural Plasticity - The ability of the brain to change and adapt in response to experience, learning, or injury, by forming new neural connections and reorganizing existing ones.

Neuroengineering - The application of engineering techniques to understand, manipulate, and enhance the functioning of the brain, often involving brain-computer interfaces, neural implants, and other technologies.

Neuroethics - A subfield of bioethics focused on the ethical issues arising from advancements in neuroscience and neurotechnology, including concerns about cognitive enhancement, free will, and privacy.

Neuroplasticity - The brain's ability to reorganize and form new neural connections throughout life, a concept that is central to understanding both cognitive development and the potential for cognitive enhancement through technological means, such as brain-computer interfaces or neurostimulation.

Post-Humanism - A philosophical movement that advocates for transcending human nature through technological, biological, or cognitive enhancement, often questioning the traditional boundaries between human beings and machines.

Posthuman Condition - A theoretical state in which human beings evolve or transform into something radically different from current biological humanity, often through the use of enhancement technologies. The posthuman condition challenges traditional notions of human identity, ethics, and society.

Privacy in Cognitive Enhancement - The right to keep one's mental and cognitive states private, particularly as new technologies allow for the manipulation of thoughts, memories, and emotions. Privacy concerns are central to discussions of the ethical limits of enhancement technologies.

Radical Life Extension - The concept of significantly extending the human lifespan through medical or technological interventions, potentially altering the natural aging process. Ethical questions arise around the implications for society, overpopulation, and the distribution of such technologies.

Self-Actualization - A psychological concept referring to the realization of one's full potential. In the context of human enhancement, it raises the question of whether enhancement technologies can assist individuals in achieving self-actualization or if they create artificial standards of human perfection.

Singularity (Technological) - A point in the future where technological growth becomes uncontrollable and irreversible, resulting in profound changes to human civilization, often involving the creation of superintelligent AI.

Superintelligence - An intelligence that exceeds human cognitive abilities in every aspect, including creativity, problem-solving, and social skills, often envisioned as a result of advanced artificial intelligence.

Synthetic Biology - An interdisciplinary field that combines biology, engineering, and computer science to design and construct new biological parts, systems, or organisms that do not exist naturally.

Technological Singularity - A hypothetical future point at which technological growth becomes uncontrollable and irreversible, resulting in unforeseeable changes to human civilization, often associated with the rise of superintelligent AI.

Transhumanism - An intellectual and cultural movement that supports the use of advanced technologies to enhance the human condition, aiming to overcome physical and mental limitations and extend human life.

References

1. Agar, N. (2010). Liberal Eugenics: In Defence of Human Enhancement. Wiley-Blackwell.

2. Aiello, L. C., & Wheeler, P. (1995). "The expensive tissue hypothesis: The brain and the digestive system in human evolution." Current Anthropology, 36(2), 199-221.

3. Aristotle. (2009). Nicomachean Ethics (W. D. Ross, Trans.). Oxford University Press. (Original work published ca. 350 BCE)

4. Baker, M. R., et al. (2018). "Neuroprosthetics: A critical review of brain-computer interface technologies." Neural Engineering, 15(2), 1-13.

5. Bentham, J. (1780). An Introduction to the Principles of Morals and Legislation. Oxford University Press.

6. Bostrom, N. (2005). "In Defense of Posthuman Dignity." Bioethics, 19(3), 202-214.

7. Bostrom, N. (2008). Directed Evolution and the Human Future. In Human Enhancement (pp. 15–35). Oxford University Press.

8. Bostrom, N. (2008). "Human enhancement: A philosophical perspective." Journal of Medicine and Philosophy, 33(5), 427-444.

9. Bostrom, N. (2014). Superintelligence: Paths, Dangers, Strategies. Oxford University Press.

10. Bostrom, N., & Sandberg, A. (2009). "Cognitive

Enhancement: Methods, Ethics, Regulatory Challenges." Science and Engineering Ethics, 15(3), 311–341.

11. Bostrom, N., & Roache, R. (2008). Ethical issues in human enhancement. Journal of Value Inquiry, 42(4), 443-457.

12. Braidotti, R. (2013). The Posthuman. Polity Press.

13. Bryson, J. R., & Castree, N. (2012). The geographical political economy of human enhancement technologies. The Geographical Journal, 178(2), 118-129.

14. Buchanan, A., Brock, D., Daniels, N., & Wikler, D. (2000). From chance to choice: Genetics and justice. Cambridge University Press.

15. Chalmers, D. J. (2021). Reality+: Virtual Worlds and the Problems of Philosophy. W. W. Norton & Company.

16. Clark, A. (2003). Natural-Born Cyborgs: Minds, Technologies, and the Future of Human Intelligence. Oxford University Press.

17. Clark, A. (2008). Supersizing the Mind: Embodiment, Action, and Cognitive Extension. Oxford University Press.

18. Clynes, M., & Kline, N. (1960). Cyborgs and Space. Astronautics, 8(1), 26–27.

19. Confucius. (2007). The Analects (D. C. Lau, Trans.). Penguin Classics. (Original work published ca. 5th–4th century BCE)

20. Descartes, R. (1637). Discourse on the Method. Hackett Publishing Company. (Original work

published 1637)

21. Dworkin, R. (2000). Sovereign Virtue: The Theory and Practice of Equality. Harvard University Press.

22. Engel, G. L. (1977). "The biopsychosocial model and the challenge of human health." Science, 196(4286), 1305-1309.

23. Foucault, M. (1976). The Birth of Biopolitics. Springer.

24. Fukuyama, F. (2002). Our Posthuman Future: Consequences of the Biotechnology Revolution. Farrar, Straus and Giroux.

25. Greenfield, S. (2011). "The human enhancement revolution: The possibilities of living better." Nature, 473(7346), 304-305.

26. Harari, Y. N. (2016). Homo Deus: A Brief History of Tomorrow. HarperCollins.

27. Harari, Y. N. (2017). Homo Deus: A Brief History of Tomorrow. Harper.

28. Haraway, D. (1991). A Cyborg Manifesto: Science, Technology, and Socialist-Feminism in the Late Twentieth Century. Routledge.

29. Harris, J. (2007). Enhancement and the Ethics of Human Flourishing. Journal of Applied Philosophy, 24(3), 263-278.

30. Harris, J. (2010). Enhancing evolution: The ethical case for making better people. Princeton University Press.

31. Hunsaker, R., et al. (2011). "Advances in prosthetics technology: Implications for rehabilitation." Disability and Rehabilitation: Assistive Technology,

6(4), 309-317.

32. Jasanoff, S. (2005). Technologies of humility: Citizen participation in governance of science. Minerva, 43(3), 223-244.

33. Joyce, G., Rozovsky, S., & McCammon, J. (2005). "Nanotechnology and Human Enhancement: A Global Perspective." Journal of Nanotechnology, 9(1), 42-55.

34. Kant, I. (1785). Groundwork for the Metaphysics of Morals. Cambridge University Press.

35. Kurzweil, R. (2005). The Singularity is Near: When Humans Transcend Biology. Penguin Books.

36. Laozi. (2009). Tao Te Ching (D. C. Lau, Trans.). Penguin Classics. (Original work published ca. 4th century BCE).

37. Locke, J. (1690). Two Treatises of Government. The Liberal Arts Press.

38. Lebedev, M. A., & Nicolelis, M. A. L. (2006). "Brain–machine interfaces: Past, present and future." Trends in Neurosciences, 29(9), 494–501.

39. Lloyd, G. E. R. (1978). Hippocratic writings. Penguin Classics.

40. Maciocia, G. (2005). The Foundations of Chinese Medicine: A Comprehensive Text for Acupuncture and Chinese Medicine Practitioners. Elsevier Health Sciences.

41. Mayer, L. (2013). "Nanotechnology in Medicine: Current State and Future Prospects." Journal of Medical Nanotechnology, 17(4), 283–295.

42. Metzinger, T. (2009). The Ego Tunnel: The Science of

the Mind and the Quest for the Self. Basic Books.

43. Miller, E. K., & Cohen, J. D. (2001). "An integrative theory of prefrontal cortex function." Annual Review of Neuroscience, 24, 167-202.

44. Moltmann, J. (1993). The Trinity and the Kingdom. Fortress Press.

45. Miah, A. (2012). Human enhancement: The challenges for public policy. Critical Social Policy, 32(4), 520-539.

46. Parfit, D. (1984). Reasons and Persons. Oxford University Press.

47. Pasquale, F. (2015). The Black Box Society: The Secret Algorithms That Control Money and Information. Harvard University Press.

48. Plato. (2003). The Republic (B. Jowett, Trans.). Dover Publications. (Original work published ca. 380 BCE)

49. Rawls, J. (1971). A Theory of Justice. Harvard University Press.

50. Riedel, S. (2005). "The history of vaccination." The Lancet Infectious Diseases, 5(7), 520-522.

51. Savulescu, J. (2001). "Genetic Interventions and the Ethics of Enhancement of Human Beings." Bioethics, 15(6), 415–435.

52. Savulescu, J., & Bostrom, N. (2009). Human Enhancement. Oxford University Press.

53. Sandel, M. (2007). The Case Against Perfection: Ethics in the Age of Genetic Engineering. Harvard University Press.

54. Singer, P. (1979). Practical Ethics. Cambridge University Press.

55. Spaemann, R. (2007). Persons: The Difference Between 'Someone' and 'Something'. Oxford University Press.

56. Tasioulas, J. (2013). Human enhancement, human nature, and the ethics of new technologies. Journal of Moral Philosophy, 10(3), 287-311.

57. Thompson, D. F. (2007). The Ethics of Autonomy. Cambridge University Press.

58. Tomasello, M. (1999). The Cultural Origins of Human Cognition. Harvard University Press.

59. Verheij, J. (2009). Autonomy and Enhancement. Journal of Medical Ethics, 35(4), 189-193.

60. Waldby, C. (2013). The Biopolitics of Human Enhancement. Palgrave Macmillan.

61. Warwick, K. (2014). "Cyborg Morals, Cyborg Ethics: Ethical Implications of Becoming a Cyborg." Ethics and Information Technology, 16(3), 219–226.

62. Weinberg, A. M. (2010). The humanities in the age of biotechnology. Technology and Culture, 51(3), 589-611.

63. Zhang, Y., & Zhu, D. (2017). Technological singularity and its potential social impact. Science and Engineering Ethics, 23(6), 1501-1520.

64. Zuboff, S. (2019). The Age of Surveillance Capitalism: The Fight for a Human Future at the New Frontier of Power. PublicAffairs.

About the Author

Joseph Demegillo is a mathematician, data scientist, and writer with a profound interest in the ethical and philosophical implications of human enhancement. His work bridges the realms of mathematics, cognitive science, and philosophy, with a particular focus on exploring the boundaries of human potential in the modern age. Through his writing, Joseph seeks to provoke thoughtful reflection on the ethical dilemmas posed by advancements in biotechnology, neuroengineering, and artificial intelligence. Growing up in a modest neighborhood in Metro Manila, Philippines, Joseph developed a deep appreciation for knowledge, nurtured by his parents' belief in its transformative power. His father's hard work and his mother's love of learning inspired him to pursue an academic path despite financial challenges. These early experiences shaped his understanding of the mind's capacity for growth and the importance of self-awareness in navigating the complexities of life.

Joseph's intellectual journey has led him to explore the intricate connections between cognition, ethics, and technological innovation. He is particularly intrigued by the potential consequences of human enhancement technologies on society and individual identity. As an advocate for critical thinking, Joseph encourages readers to consider both the promises and the pitfalls of altering the human condition. In addition to his academic pursuits, Joseph is the founder of

Prodigy Digital, a platform dedicated to sharing thought-provoking ideas through eBooks, articles, and other media. His work combines rigorous analysis with a deep appreciation for the nuances of human experience, encouraging readers to engage with complex issues and embrace the unknown with curiosity and open-mindedness.

Through Beyond the Flesh: The Ethics of Enhancement, Joseph invites readers to reflect on the future of humanity in an era of rapid technological change, urging them to confront the ethical questions that accompany the power to transcend our biological limitations.

Don't miss out!

Visit the website below and you can sign up to receive emails whenever joseph demegillo publishes a new book. There's no charge and no obligation.

https://books2read.com/r/B-A-TKLUC-GYRIF

BOOKS2READ

Connecting independent readers to independent writers.